Empowerment through coaching, a strategy for leaders

Empowerment through coaching, a strategy for leaders

JD Roman
Manuel Ferrández

Olibros
en red

www.librosenred.com

C.E.O.: Marcelo Perazolo
Managing Editor: Ivana Basset
Cover Design: Daniela Ferrán
Interior Design: Federico de Giacomi

Design, typesetting, and other prepress work by LibrosEnRed
www.librosenred.com

ISBN: 978-1-59754-405-4

First English Edition - Print on Demand

LibrosEnRed©
A trade mark of Amertown International S.A.
editorial@librosenred.com

TABLE OF CONTENTS

Prologue

Many many years ago, in a far far away country, the current prime minister publicly boasted his full knowledge of what Socrates had written (the ancient Greek philosopher, not the famous Brazilian soccer player of the 70s).

Such a labor should not have consumed too much of his valuable time, as Socrates didn't write anything at all; well, at least nothing that has survived the passing of centuries. (By the way, he was re-elected for a second term, the PM, not Socrates. This demonstrates that a total lack of culture, or ridicule, is no serious impairment for leading a country).

But let's cut to the chase, i.e. coaching and its historical roots.

Everything we know of Socrates, we know thanks to the writings of his disciples; Plato, amongst others.

And, nevertheless, the founding father of coaching is the very Socrates, detail that we discovered accidentally many years ago, in Geneva, Switzerland, when a top manager wondered how we could be so "naturally" Socratic. At that moment, we thought that tagging someone as Socratic was some kind of scorn, but we remained deadpan; and instead of publicly exposing our lack of knowledge and making a fool of ourselves, we started investigating about coaching.

And we discovered that, the same way Molière's Mr.Jourdain was unconsciously doing prose, we had been practicing Socratic coaching for many years.

Why was it possible? The fact is that our main specialties are coaching and training, whether of the classic kind, in classroom; or of the so-called outdoor and experiential kind. In that later modality, the Socratic approach, albeit unknown to us at that time, turns out to be an indispensable transmission vector.

And so, all in all, it turns out that, totally unaware of the fact, for decades we had been "Socraticaly coaching" people all throughout the world.

For whom? For many of the number one companies: in automotive, IT, pharmacy, or in luxury and fashion related industries. We must occult their names, as our clients don't wish to go public about the coaching projects they currently develop.

Basically, this obeys to a very simple reason: coaching, for them, is a strategic tool, a tool that has helped them reach the top and, moreover, remain there.

Here, let's be a little bit cautious. Provided that the term "coaching" has become pretty fashionable, it seems that nowadays every man and his dog are doing coaching, even on the more ludicrous or irrelevant topics, let's talk a bit about the term "coaching" and about what it means.

But, prior to beginning, we want to ponder for a while a topic that's often left aside: the ROI (return on investment) of a coaching process. More precisely, how much do I get out of a coaching process, what are the benefits, and more tangibly, what's the measurable profit I can reasonably expect from the same? With no doubt, coaching generates results, but it's compulsory to gauge them. As well, coaching has a cost, and obviously, it's necessary to measure it.

We're already putting forward some concepts that we will profusely analyze. It's about using quantitative and qualitative metrics, definitely, but it's worth walking an extra step: how can we translate the qualitative results into quantitative results? This step turns out to be really tricky, truth to be said, and, maybe for that reason, often remains left aside or plainly dismissed with positive, and utterly void, sentences like this:

> "Coaching will help us work on the improvement of self-esteem, work environment, psychological state of mind of our employees, and so on and so on … "

For us, this kind of statement is meaningless. If someone decides to invest in coaching, the natural reaction would be that he wants to know, well, he should, tangibly how much that action is going to pay back. Period.

Here, some hint: if we want to know what's the contribution of a coaching process to our overall business, probably we should come to methodologies similar to pharmaceutical analysis, with "double-blind" tests.

This means that we pick a homogeneous group of people and perform coaching with only half of the group.

Obviously, it's vital that the other half DOESN'T KNOW that a coaching process is under way, because that very knowledge, through induction, would contaminate that half-group.

Anyway, being positive, whether such a thing would happen, it nevertheless would multiply the impact of the program. Although, as a drawback, obviously that would impede the correct reading and measurement of the actual impact of the ongoing coaching process. We would be back to square one, unable to measure the impact of the ongoing coaching process.

We will come back later on this aspect of coaching, which seems vital to us. But by now, we're going to treat of the sheer technical aspects of coaching.

In several occasions, we will refer to some of our already published books where we have penetrated concepts that constitute the substratum for developing coaching programs. For instance, "The paper bridge", which deals with training methodology and with how we acquire knowledge. Also, "The communication man", which carries out a revision to all the skills required for a proper one-to-one communication, indispensable for coaching.

On the other hand, we want to give some room to the different interpretations that are broadcasted on the concept of coaching. Thus, we will try to give some turns of the screw to the concept, examining it from different angles and points of view.

Added to that, we will always use the term of coachee when referring to the individual who's undergoing a coaching process, whether already initiated or on the verge of beginning.

Also, beyond the fashionable aspect, which undoubtedly it's important to bear in mind, we will see that coaching is linked to the economical and management environment and to the new conditions that force the companies introduce new strategic paradigms.

By instance, how can we measure something as intangible as an "excellent environment of work"? What actions may reveal that we indeed exceed the expectations of our customers? However, as demanding as it may seem at first glance, measuring the cultural values and their development doesn't turn out to be impossible.

We all know what it's required to do in our job, more or less, it is convenient to bear in mind this aspect when we initiate a coaching process, and not assume "obvious" things.

But, what happens if what we need to work at is something intangible, i.e. some cultural value that we all have to demonstrate in order for the company, and ourselves, by the way, to triumph?

Most companies define their cultural values attending to a strategic imperative. If the strategic imperative takes root in centering on the customer, the culture must centre on parameters that foment the satisfaction, or exceeds the satisfaction, of the customer. If the vision consists of developing close alliances, the key value would be related to irreproachable ethics.

Defining cultural values turns out to be simple enough. Even it's possible to obtain that people act accordingly so. Nevertheless, measuring whether such behaviors have managed to penetrate the culture of the company, and whether the company does what it publicly boasts, etc. that's an authentic challenge.

The companies habitually use human resources tools and indicators to gauge up to what point the individual performance of its people support the overall results of the company. For instance, the production managers use to be evaluated depending on their aptitude to increase the production levels and reduce the costs. They are rewarded depending on the fulfillment of goals, quantitative, and they are penalized if they don't deliver. This facet we call it the WHAT.

Nevertheless, it is vital to measure something more than the mere operative results of business. The conventional systems of performance measurement tend to forget how the task is performed and how the results are obtained. This is the HOW.

It turns out that, ultimately, the HOW has an impact on the profits, the WHAT.

And finally, thus far, we will profusely talk about leadership; as coaching and leadership are intimately entwined; coaching being one of the most powerful development tool for an operative leader, i.e. a leader with people reporting to him, people he has the responsibility of helping grow as professionals; this later facet constituting an important way of establishing or consolidating actual leadership with his people.

And so, this is what we're going to talk about: I can be a leader at my workplace, but I will need to apply some techniques that can boost my leadership capacity. And it happens that one of them, we think one of the most powerful, is precisely coaching.

In acting accordingly so, people will follow me, one of the basic characteristics of leaders, not only because of the foreseeable outcome, or benefits, they will get from their allegiance, so far wishful thinking or sheer faith, but also, and especially, because of the tangible personal benefits they can get here and now, as a consequence of what coaching can bring them.

Once those premises are properly set, let's start now with our trip through leadership and coaching concepts. You will recognize most of them, you will downright miss some of them, or in any case you will miss some keener insight on for instance classical motivational theories, but we thought it was much more suitable to focus on what we personally deem as more important, and to ensure that those facets are covered from any possible angle we could come up with.

1 - The basics

INTRODUCTION

The global economy has altered "the rules of the game". Nowadays, the companies cannot allow the luxury of controlling everything from the top management point of view. The companies that are successful, the best of them, are those that can rapidly answer to changes in the markets, in the new technologies, in governmental policy and in the new social attitudes.

This capacity for change cannot be programmed inside classic systems and procedures.

The fundamental aspects that determine the development of the companies are the quality of their leaders. (Here we already hint that a coach has first to be a leader. Hence the title of the book).

So far, many people have opened some debate about whether the leader is born, nature, or is made, nurture. Let's make it clear, once and for all: a negligible minority "is born" with that skill and an overwhelming majority is **not** born with that skill.

Hence it's compulsory, and possible, to develop that skill, period. Later on, anyway, we will talk more in depth about the notions of leader and leadership and their utmost importance in any coaching process. Though we can already give a hint about another key aspect of coaching, and of the figure of the coach, and it's that because of the non-hierarchic relation that exists between the coach and the "coachee", even when the coach is a superior of the coachee, the "leadership" skill, individual leadership, not public leadership, turns out to be fundamental.

A former, and externally imposed to us, colleague of ours, we stopped working with him as soon as we had the chance, never walked that stretch. Whenever a meeting was taking place, he beforehand told everybody that he wanted to be the leader of the meeting. Whenever we had to practice coaching with somebody, he boasted that he was the most suitable professional for performing it, and so on, and so on. He was both absolutely confused and definitively obsessed with leadership, especially because, although he would never come to confessing it aloud, nobody paid any attention to his pretenses. He was confusing the fact of being aggressive and vehement with being seen as a leader, what increased his frustration even more. He had no natural gift for leadership, although he wasn't aware of it, and he had not the inner desire to develop such a skill, obviously because his lack of self-criticism prevented him from facing the truth. Needless to say that such an obnoxious behavior produced rejection both in his colleagues, us, and in his would-be coachees.

So, in order to close the already expected debate, we are convinced that leadership is a skill, or a bundle of skills, and hence can be developed, like any other "soft skill". Obviously, we agree on the obvious part, that is that depending on our personal starting point, nature, we will, through nurture, progress higher and quicker than others; or lower and slower, for that matter.

Let's move ahead then.

Let's start with some basic concepts, which are going to help us along our trip in the world of coaching, as a powerful tool for a leader in times of permanent change.

The three key words around which spins the whole book could be concentrated in a sentence like this: change and how a leader can confront it, focused on the people development through the use of a coaching process.

But, first of all, let's see what coaching is NOT.

What coaching is NOT

It turns out obvious that, despite the multitude of changes occurring in the business world, most managers have not substantially modified their way of acting. Many people don't have an accurate idea of what, in practice, means "coaching". Therefore, coaching turns into one of those fashionable ideas, which, in practice, are often discarded with contempt. Nevertheless, coaching is no magic, so hereafter we want to wipe out some erroneous concepts.

1 - Coaching cannot be defined

Actually, coaching is a well-defined process, which possesses a starting point and a finishing line. What's different is that the heart of the process is the potential of the person. That's why it's so demanding to gauge; although, as we already anticipated, it's not impossible.

2 - Coaching is psychotherapy

Frequently, managers elude initiating a coaching process because they are afraid that entering that unfamiliar world demands them to turn into some kind of psychologist. They surmise that they will have to dive into the darkest inner secrets of the coachee. Actually, somehow, they must appeal to some basic psychological tools in order to deal with the behaviors they might encounter. But having studied psychology is not a compulsory requirement for being a good coach. It's just necessary to be prepared for managing personal and emotional questions. Truth to be said, it's not that easy, because normally our education, typically business or technical education, has not prepared us for that; but let's not relinquish any hope.

3 - Coaching is about making people feel happy

Many managers think that coaching means doing what they already do, but taking in account the "feelings" of their people, due to the fact that when they are required to do coaching, they center on the human being. Actually, although managing is, simplifying to the max, making people do things, coaching consists of helping the individuals manage the problems by themselves. As a collateral effect, it is most true that they will be more happy and motivated, but that was not the initially intended outcome.

4 - Coaching and mentoring are the same thing

A coach doesn't construct emotional links. A mentor does. If someone doesn't fulfill a commitment, a mentor might say: "You have disappointed me". On the other hand, in the same situation, a coach would say: "This is what you said you would do, and you are not doing it". Coaching always sustains on sheer facts.

5 - A coach is someone who encourages

Any coaching process begins with an analysis, shared, of the strong points and of the improvement points. Coaching is very much orientated to action. A coach doesn't only praise the efforts; he helps his coachees understand what they have to change in order to reach their professional goals. So, sometimes he praises the positive outcome of a specific action, and sometimes he highlights what has not been done and where posterior efforts are to be put.

6 - Coaching demands a lot of time and resources

Managers dread that coaching is very demanding in terms of time, and consequently that diverts them from initiating such a process. But, for a good manager it will be enough to devote five odd percent of his labor day to coaching work. And finally, he will discover that this effort, seen as an investment, eventually helps him save time. In the long term, the remuneration is high. You help the individuals understand and integrate how to solve their problems by themselves. A coaching process can last between three months and two years, true, but it's a part-time job, and it depends on what we want to obtain from the coachee.

7 - It applies to all kinds of situations and businesses

Well, it depends... Actually, a magic recipe doesn't exist. Later on, we will explore what circumstances are the most appropriate and what are not. We can already hint that this has to see with the motivation, according to Maslow's pyramid, level of the person at a specific moment.

8 - Not everybody can receive coaching

If a relation of coaching doesn't work, for instance, if anybody involved in such a process doesn't respond as expected, probably it's due to the fact that the coach is making the wrong moves. But if eventually coaching really doesn't work, it's compulsory to discover what blocks the coachee, without assuming that the whole responsibility belongs to him. If someone doesn't respond to a coaching process, probably some problems exist in the relation. Before assuming that it's impossible to fix it, it would be suitable to change coach.

9 - The well-trained coachees will leave the company

Some managers are afraid that if they help someone develop himself and reach his professional goals, this will inspire that individual to look for new horizons. It's most true that some individuals will want to leave and, whatever their motive, it will be impossible to stop them. However, all human beings possess hidden resources. As soon as they start discovering them, realizing how they can use them within their current company, they get enthusiastic and therefore are less prone to look for external adventures.

Though it's always possible that some employees might leave the company in a quest for new challenges, many others will feel indebted with the company and will be more faithful to a company that's interested in the professional development of its employees. And that's not just positive thinking.

10 - Coaching is not concerned by profitability

Here it's important to be careful. We were commenting on it initially, do you remember? We talked about the ROI of coaching.

Many managers consider coaching to be a "minor skill"; i.e. something that doesn't produce an immediate rise in the figures. Actually, coaching generates results, notably more consistent than many other people management approaches.

From a qualitative point of view, the HOW, coaching develops creativity in the individuals. It encourages them to be more flexible, to adapt themselves to new situations. And the response from the coachees can induce, without any kind of doubts, a substantial effect on the income of a company. Nevertheless, it's also true that it's important to optimize the resources devoted to coaching. They must be those, which, time given, will provoke a great impact in the company. Coaching supposes an investment in someone; and it will provide real results, but not in the short term.

When you give support to someone simply in order for that individual to reach the next month sales target, this is not coaching, although some would call it coaching. But if this individual is a sales consultant with a high potential and you help him develop his own sales methodology, not only with the WHAT, but also with the HOW, then it's coaching. Coaching can have a positive impact on the results of the company, but hardly in the short term, namely one month. Because of this, it's important to focus on those individuals who will turn out to be important assets for the company.

Nevertheless, in some coaching programs we have developed, measurable results, more and better sales, were attained in slightly less than 3 months.

But let's remember what the ancient Chinese philosophers used to do: they taught people how to fish, instead of feeding them with fishes.

THE POWER OF COACHING

It is clear that coaching is one of the critical skills for contemporary leadership. Due to the so deep and rapid changes that are taking place, the leader needs to generate and apply a learning and empowerment methodology that answers to those new requirements.

Coaching fits perfectly into this new model of learning, as it allows the leader to learn, modify and apply an approach adapted to a specific management situation.

When a manager receives coaching, or works as a coach, it's important to bear in mind specific aspects to heighten his efficiency: to focus both on the business and on the human talent, to generate confidence and credibility, to inspire, to look for excellence, to develop coaching as a standard process and not just as something punctual.

ALWAYS THINK ABOUT THE ROI
OF A COACHING PROCESS

Contemplate with clarity the existing relation between the above-mentioned skill and the results desired by the company.

The leaders who do coaching:
- Generate more loyalty, what means a higher loyalty from the employees

- Communicate their expectations of constant improvement, which drives their coachees improve their performance and productivity.
- Are best informed about the problems and issues of the company
- Create a labor climate where exists an open, direct communication and a culture where the problems are confronted and are quickly solved, as the individuals tend to share the information.

A real leader determines the results the company expects and thus helps his reports seek, and attain, higher goals. The real leaders help the individuals get out of a trouble by themselves. This makes sense, especially, when a leader perceives in them a much bigger potential than he was expecting.

The main challenge companies face takes root in the individuals. In a highly competitive and changing context, most of the companies look for efficiency and continuous improvement, and they are therefore submitted to high requirements in order to reach success. In that context, it is vital for them companies to develop teams that can face those challenges and are capable of moving into sceneries of uncertainty. The above-mentioned responsibility relapses on managers who, often, have to produce results beyond what they are, or deemed as, capable of.

In the same line, the managers are to develop their skills, to understand the organizational and human phenomena, to develop new learning capacities and to attain positive states of mind.

On the other hand, managers are submitted to a diversity of requirements and commitments, with goals always more demanding. They generate high expectations that, often, originate stress or depression. The individuals tend to work beyond what they can, to give more than they have and to take charge of problems for which they not have the necessary skills.

All of those requirements, both external and internal, cause the environment to fill up a sense of weariness, often adorned with family and personal problems. Surely, all this is due to the fact that the speed with which knowledge advances, in any area, implies that what we can do in a specific moment can become very quickly obsolete.

Some companies choose to ignore the situation and others choose simply to rotate their personnel when they detect that there are some "burnt out" individuals. Nevertheless, the current trend is that the intelligent companies centre on teamwork, showing interest for the individuals, and giving feedback. That's to say, in other words, applying a coaching process.

During that process, the relation that the coach establishes is based on the respect for the other, so that he never adopts an attitude of superiority. The coach suggests the coachee the idea of a change and helps him preserve what's working well and transform what doesn't serve. Besides, he worries for promoting the process over the results in the short term. As well, the coach will open the coachee to the observation of a new range of options and solutions to the problems.

The coach helps see the costs and the benefits of a promotion, a position change or the acquisition of any new level of responsibility, leaving in plain view both costs and benefits observed from different perspectives.

In this process, ethics represent a fundamental matter. The definition of what are the values a company seeks and takes care of can help the coachees understand how those values match their owns. The orientation of coaching is, therefore, to obtain an opening of conscience, a development of the skills, a managing of the states of mind and implementation of practices, likewise the support for the acquisition of suitable behaviors and attitudes.

As it is known, Maieutics was the method Socrates used to extracting from his interlocutors the knowledge they harbored and that had not blossomed yet. The same method is the one that coaches use with managers: they expose their whole personal and professional potential; helping them to learn, in order that they can find by themselves the solution to their problems.

Nevertheless, it's not compulsory to think of the coach as the sole individual in charge of management development, but as that individual that helps the manager self-develop: the coach doesn't say what it's compulsory for exercising people management. What indeed does a coach is formulate questions that allow the critical reflection of his interlocutor. Reflection about what he does well and, especially, about what it's important to change in his management style.

Some specialists define management coaching as "the accompaniment of an individual or a team for the development of their personal and technical knowledge potential". This definition covers the concept of accompaniment and, at the same time, specifies the area of coaching: the professional needs. It eliminates the private needs, what allow us distinctly distinguish coaching from psychotherapy.

Some basic concepts

Let's cast a glance now at some basic technical aspects.

Coaching is a system that includes concepts, structures, processes, tools and measurement instruments. It also implies applying a tangible style of leadership.

Coaching relies on conversations, not on mere chats.

It uses the positive feedback based on observation.

Coaching opens windows to explore new concepts, systems, skills, tools and management technologies that focus on:

- A methodology built around strategies and tactics that always aim towards a major management vision.
- An integral, consistent, constant system, for the development of the individual talents at their workplace.
- A teamwork system that promotes the individual skills aiming at better results for the whole team.
- An approach that transforms the current work into training and development.

Basic characteristics of coaching

Essentially five basic characteristics exist:

1 - The vision is tangible. Based on facts.

Coaching focuses on behaviors that can be improved. It focuses on the objective and descriptive aspects of performance. Performance can be improved only when it can be described in a precise and unmisunderstandable way, when both parts actually understand the same thing.

2 - Interactivity.
The one who talks the most should be the coachee.

In the coaching conversations information is interchanged. Questions are asked and answers given, ideas are interchanged.

3 - The responsibility is shared. Not only by the coach.

The coach, as well as the coachee, holds a shared responsibility in the constant improvement of performance. Both parts share the responsibility for achieving that the conversation ensues the maximum possible usefulness.

4 - The way, or process, is specific. A structure exists

The way is determined by two basic factors: first, the goal of the conversation is distinctly defined. And second, the flow of the conversation respects some distinctly defined steps.

5 - Respect is permanent.
The most important thing is the coachee

The coach communicates, at all time, his respect for the individual who receives coaching.

SOME BASIC ELEMENTS OF COACHING

Values

Coaching possesses as fundamental basis the values that already have been discussed. Not being so, it would turn out in being little less than the exhibition of a series of tricks.

Results

Coaching is a process orientated to results that assume the constant performance improvement as a consequence, be it individual or as a group.

Discipline

Coaching is a disciplinary interaction. In order to really stick to the constant improvement approach, a coach must be sufficiently disciplined to create the essential conditions for success.

Prior training

To tackle coaching, training is needed. Intuitive knowledge or simple memorization of ideas and concepts is not enough.

When can we give coaching?

Coaching can apply when:

- Exists a poor or deficient feedback on the progress of the employees, accompanied by a low labour performance.
- An employee in any area deserves to be congratulated for the exemplary execution of some skill.
- The employee needs to improve some skill at his workplace.

The efficient coaching is the one that is characterized by positivism and confidence.

How does coaching work?

Coaching works through a conversation where mutual commitments appear.

- From the coachee: Commitment to obtain a top result, honesty with what happens and disposition towards achievement.
- From the coach: Commitment that the result of his coachee will be bigger than what the coachee would achieve on his own.

Note that in some occasions, coaches also work with attitude problems, although never falling in the trap of false or cheap psychology.

Therefore, when a company wants to obtain results that were never obtained before, or results different from what their personal history would allow them to obtain, it is in an excellent moment for contracting a coach.

Qualitative and quantitative

We will examine some of the qualitative reasons, why coaching is important for the companies:

- It facilitates that the individuals adapt to changes in an efficient way.
- It mobilizes the central values and commitments of the human being.
- It stimulates the individuals towards the production of unprecedented results
- It refreshes and updates relation nets and makes communication more efficient.
- It predisposes the individuals towards collaboration, teamwork and creation of consensus.
- It unveils the potential of the individuals, allowing them to reach goals that otherwise would be considered as unattainable.

Quantitative reasons.

Coaching is very much centered on results (an increase in sales figures for instance), but to the coaches what really matters is the individuals; in the end, as they are those who produce the results. The power in a relation of coaching doesn't take root in the authority of the coach, but in the commitment and the vision of the individuals. The coaches give the power to the individuals.

Who's the coach?

The coach is not only a figure who worries for planning the personal and professional growth of the individuals. From this point of view, the coach is, undoubtedly, a leader, or at least he harbors many qualities usually associated with leaders.

He possesses an inspiring, winning and transcendent vision, which, through example, discipline, responsibility and commitment, encourages the individuals to walk towards a vision. In order to accompany the individual in that trip, a series of compulsory elements are to be present, which we detail hereafter.

- **Communication**: A coach has to be thorough with his communication.
- **Support**: That means supporting the team, contributing with any help the coachee might need, whether with information, with materials, with advices or, simply, showing understanding.
- **Confidence**: The individuals should be convinced that the coach believes in them. He checks with them the reasons of success and provides recognition.
- **Shared vision:** This means sharing a vision about the common goals. The key is to insure that his interlocutors can answer such questions as: why is this goal so important for the group or for the company? What steps must we walk to reach the goals?, when, etc …?
- **Empathy:** That supposes understanding the point of view of the coachees. Asking questions to interact with the individuals, questions that reveal their reality. Never assume that we already know what the coachees feel.
- **Remuneration / punishment:** This means ensuring that people know with specificity that mistakes are not going to be punished, (provided that they eventually learn from them).
- **Patience:** time and patience turn out to be key factors for preventing the coach of reacting too fast.
- **Discretion:** The best coaches are those that manage to guarantee confidentiality, which constitutes the basis of confidence and eventually, of their credibility as leaders.

- **Respect:** It's the attitude towards the individuals per-ceived in the manager. A manager may respect the members of his team, but if this attitude is in contradic-tion with a disposition to interact, then this does convey little respect.

And it's that the coaches perform many tasks: they advise, they establish direction and provide feedback. They propose tasks that develop the skills and help reach success. About success, they reach it anticipating the problems and poten-tial obstacles that the coachees will face, as well as helping them get the necessary resources. This implies that they help their coachees accept failure and embrace success. Actually, by helping them around obstacles and by assigning the adequate resources, the good coaches promote success.

Functions of the coach:

Amongst the main characteristics we find:
- Visionary and inspiring leadership.
- Picker of talents.
- Coach of teams.
- Accompaniment of coachees in real situations.
- Coach of the individual performances
- Motivator and mentor of career development.
- Inspirer of teamwork.
- Innovative strategist.

Other basic conducts for the coach

- **Active listening**: This term refers to the behaviors and attitudes that the coaches put into gear in order to con-vey that they are actually listening. In this activity, are involved verbal and non-verbal aspects (see the cor-responding chapter in the book "The communication man"). Probably the main skill is the skill of listening without evaluating immediately or with haste what our interlocutor is saying. This implies trying to understand what our interlocutor is trying to convey, instead of evaluating if what he says is correct or incorrect or of if we agree or not.

- **Compiling information:** For the coach it's important to be capable of compiling the sufficient information to obtain positive results. Coaches can help people solve problems, aware of the way those individuals understand their problem, what they have already done to solve it and how they think that those problems can be resolved.
- **To re-formulate**: Another behavior that helps the coach obtain information is reformulation. That way, we convey that we're actually listening, that we understand what our interlocutor says or feels, and that we are not judging him. To re-formulate means expressing in other words what we believe our interlocutor has said and to understand the feelings that our interlocutor has expressed.
- **Support:** This tool focus on the final result of coaching: the continuous improvement in the learning process. It expresses the coach conviction of his desire that the individual improves his competences. It supports the sense of achievement in our interlocutor and contributes to the commitment to constant improvement. Always bearing in mind that there are two groups of skills demonstrated by the person: the skills that the individual has demonstrated at his workplace and those that the individual shows during a coaching conversation.
- **Self-responsibility:** Means assuming the responsibility of his own behavior and accepting the responsibility for the result of the coaching interaction.
- **Managing and leading:** The coaches have a commitment towards a top performance.

Giving orders is not leadership. As such a behavior doesn't lead towards a commitment with a top performance or towards constant improvement and better performance.

An ideal performance is the result of the individuals' commitment to get the best out of them. This commitment is one of the consequences of the following pre-conditions:

- The individuals understand what they are doing and why it is important.
- The individuals possess the skills to achieve the tasks that are expected from them.
- The individuals feel valued by what they do.
- The individuals feel challenged by their jobs.
- The individuals have the opportunity to improve when they commit mistakes.

THE FIRST SCHEME OF FUNCTIONING

Coaching can be seen as a process in three stages:

1 - Preparation
Contact with the company and with the coachee. Here is where the context is analyzed and goals are defined.

2 - Coaching conversations
Meetings between the coachee and the coach in order to explore the current situation, to design an action plan that leads the coachee to reaching his goals.

3 - Follow-up
The coach verifies the fulfillment of the goals by his interlocutor and the improvements obtained by him. From there on, future actions are planned.

There would be six stages for initiating a classic coaching process.

1. Explain the intention and the importance of the process
2. Explain the processes and the skills that the coachee has to use.
3. Show the individual how it's done.
4. Observe while the coachee practices with the process.
5. Provide feedback immediately and specifically, whether to correct mistakes or to support successes.
6. Express confidence in that the individual will reach success.

Later, we will examine how this basic model can be developed in more depth.

What it is and how it's done

Now, let's talk about the company, which is the playfield for coaching processes. As we mentioned in the prologue, there are other areas for coaching, but we focus on coaching for business.

We need the manager to develop, both professionally and personally. And, it's clear that this personalized development has an impact at all the levels in the company.

What really does the coach is to raise questions, avoiding identifying himself as an expert, because actually the one who really possesses the answers to a given situation, is the individual who's living that specific and personal situation.

We have already stressed that coaching is not about therapy. The goal of coaching is not to modify the personality of the coachee, not even his personal, affective life, etc., though, sometimes this happens as a collateral consequence, but making him work better as a manager. Hence, coaching helps modify behaviors, not personalities.

Coaching is destined principally to:

- Anybody with a responsibility inside a company.
- Anybody considered "key", not only from an objective point of view, but also from a subjective point of view.

Why coaching?

Because of the sensation that some managers have of being overwhelmed by the new challenges the company has to assume.

For the constant need to reduce costs, to increase productivity and to improve the service to the client.

For the constant pressure they have to suffer day after day.

For the isolation that they experience for not having shared their concerns with their interlocutors. Why? Because one of their main tasks is to protect them from dread, to convey safety and to motivate them; and second, because it's demanding for most of us to admit that exist challenges and responsibilities that exceed our possibilities.

Because when it comes to applying "soft" and social skills, sometimes we are not as competent as with the "hard ones".

For the need that any company has to be constantly increasing productivity.

COACHING VERSUS OTHER KINDS OF TRAINING

The first and more important advantage of coaching resides in is its own condition of a "One To One" interaction.

That way, the manager doesn't feel exposed to a public scrutiny, as it could happen during group trainings, and so the legitimate dread that his image could be damaged disappears.

Thus coaching develops in a climate of absolute confidence and confidentiality. Hence, during a session of coaching, all topics can be touched.

Often being an individual alien to the company, the coach helps develop a suitable perception of reality and helps that the individual is seen from a wider and less individual perspective when it comes to approaching different situations. All this leads to the search of solutions from other points of view previously not contemplated.

Preceding conditions inside the company:

It is desirable to, in any company that wishes an efficient application of a coaching process for its managers, organize a training session on leadership, in order to clarify some criteria in advance.

Theoretical profile of the coach

- Ample knowledge of the business world.
- Aptitude for generating a confidence relation, through credibility (that's obtained only through honesty), assertiveness, and comprehension...
- He has to be a good communicator and have well-developed communication skills, especially in active listening.
- Important analysis capacity as well as an aptitude for generating a plan for personalized and efficient development.
- Aptitude for finding, not just the suitable answers, but also the suitable questions to the different situations that he or his client could rise.
- Aptitude for finding opportunities in the "small" day-to-day actions and not only in some large management plans.
- Aptitude for grabbing and bearing in mind the organizational variables that govern the company culture, which determine the context where he can develop his performance as a coach.
- Perspicacity for bearing in mind the goals and personal values of the managers on behalf of whom he acts, as well as his own.
- Aptitude to appear as a model of confidence, communication, motivation and direction.

How can we develop a coaching process?

The election of the involved managers is fundamental for the company. We must also ensure that they have the interest of fulfilling a coaching development process. The interested parties will always have to agree on participating in the process, which, on another hand, will require an additional workload from them and some new commitments with their professional improvement.

The first conversations:

Accomplishment of a tangible diagnosis that details the so far acquired level of the sought after skills in the mentioned manager. This diagnosis will be carried out by means of personal conversation and, in some occasions, by a series of questionnaires. One of those questionnaires gauges the level of development that the individual has reached in each of his management habits; with the exception of the self-development skill, where we will use a personality questionnaire.

The above-mentioned diagnosis, obviously, is always personal and absolutely confidential, and is established only for the individual who's going to undergo the coaching process.

Feedback conversation

The coach will ask the manager to explain him what has been observed, the habits that he has developed so far in a more or less ideal way and some others that he has yet to improve. The purpose of this conversation is to contrast whether the coachee has the same perception of his situation and if he agrees to concretely work on those points. In case of any lack of coincidence in the points of view, it would be necessary to continue talking with this individual in order to analyze what specific habits he thinks he should improve.

In that conversation, some instructions are given him so he can personally elaborates his own Development Plan.

Come to this point, the conversations could be one hour and a half duration or, sometimes, even more (diagnosis conversation, diagnosis validation of goals establishment)

Development conversations

From there on, will follow a series of conversations of about an hour, with a monthly interval. Those conversations will be thoroughly devoted to work on the proposed goals. They will also be unfolding step by step, putting into practice, checking progress and, in sum, will serve to confirm that the planned action plan is efficient or not.

The coach always remains at the coachee's disposal, through e-mail, for instance, but within a prearranged frame; otherwise, the coach turns into a confessor, or into a therapist; what's fine, but those roles have nothing to do with coaching.

The whole project shouldn't extend over one year, although with some flexibility, according to the needs. Or, it shouldn't exceed 5 conversations, although again with flexibility, depending n the specific detected need.

Never forget that coaching has a definite purpose. Sometimes when the coachee feels good about the coaching conversations, he can be prone to extend the process beyond the initially accorded planning. This has to be avoided at all costs, otherwise the coaching conversations turn into some cheap therapy sessions.

In fact, the individuals who need therapy don't tend to be good candidates for coaching

And, as we already prompted out, therapy is not the purpose of coaching. Coaching has to remain a tool that companies use to developing their managers.

Management Coaching

So we have to be pragmatic. Sometimes the notion of coaching goes beyond the pure and untainted socratic approach and turns into what we call management coaching, which is a less socratic approach; but it happens that sometimes, for reasons of cost, time and management culture, this later might constitute the only available strategy that at that very moment can be put into practice.

Obviously, it's only an option, provided that we don't self-deceive thinking that we are doing "pure" coaching. Anyway, if that's the only option, we can go for it, although maybe altering a little the name, in order not to confuse people.

The companies that are using coaches to help their top management be more efficient must plan their own courses. Nobody has demonstrated yet in a conclusive way what makes a management coach suitable. Many alleged management coaches know little about business and, even sometimes, don't know too much about coaching.

Historically, for centuries, the companies prospered while they were treating their employees as mere annoying commodities. In that context, the employees were "laborers", a condition close to the very one of horses or oxen.

What might be called the re-humanization of the people began in the decade of the 70s, when successive waves of change, including globalization, an increasing demand for services, and the acceleration and restructuring of the management processes by means of the information technology, put the until then traditional companies in a dire position.

In parallel, the managers from some "leaner" and dynamic companies started recognizing the need to rely on a subtler set of skills: the communication and relation skills, indispensable to influence and infuse energy to the employees, speeding up the adaptability for the rapid change and the need for respect for the individuals hailing from always increasingly diverse backgrounds. Today, the managers expect and need some specific emotional intelligence with their supervisors and colleagues.

In spite of the whole progress achieved in other disciplines about business techniques, the current companies are still poorly equipped to solve many dilemmas related to their personnel.

DIFFERENCES

Management coaching somehow differs from other kinds of coaching. Here, our role consists in helping the "coachees", the individuals who receive coaching, produce quick business results for their bosses. So we could say that management coaching is somewhat more straightforward in its style than "classical" coaching, meaning that we work solely focused on the business metrics of the company. True, that might be deemed as contradictory in terms, when we are so obsessed in putting human beings in the foreground, but whenever at the same time we develop our interlocutors' skills, we can accept that this approach is somewhat acceptable.

The most significant element of such an approach has to deal with the fact that we use supporting tools, like predefined checklist and standard questionnaires, what forces us into working within a stricter frame for the whole process. We must admit that this approach, that we have been actually practicing, is quite suitable when doing coaching with sales teams for instance, where people are used to straightforward approaches and short-term results.

Anyway, it turns out to be remarkable to see how many intelligent individuals, motivated and in charge, rarely pause to meditate and analyze their own behaviors. More prone to head forward that to think in depth, the managers can reach high organizational spheres without having approached their own limitations. Coaching succeeds in making them lower their pace, helping them acquire conscience and perceive the effects of their words and actions. Those skills allow them perceive alternatives instead of merely react to events.

Coaching, same as any other development tool doesn't end with self-consciousness. It's a way of active learning that transfers essential communication and relation kills. The strategic coaching should integrate the personal development and the organizational needs.

Management coaching consists of extremely personal interventions, performed both in-group and in an individual way, and uses to span over several months. This coaching is fundamentally a business offer. Its intention is to produce learning, change in behavior and growth in the individual for the economic benefit of the company that uses it. We all are deeply committed in helping people live better lives, but coaching is successful only when this benefit takes place as an additional help to the business results.

Coaching constructs a triangular relation between the coach that offers the service, the coachee that receives it and the client who pays the invoices. The client is, actually, a group that includes the coachee's boss and the Human Resources department. The project is bound to success when all involved parties agree on goals that promote genuinely their own interests, as well as the common wealth.

Before picking a supplier, any potential client must examine him and thoroughly ask him what is the object of the coaching program. Companies can embrace coaching without having any pre-conceived plan. Maybe a top manager reads about coaching and decides to try it unilaterally. Or maybe Human Resources coordinates coaching for those individuals who are in a critical situation. That's why we say that management coaching has somehow a more direct and short-term vision than standard coaching.

In any case, it is critical to be clear on what are the important goals we want to reach through coaching. If you wish that coaching promotes strategic goals or inculcates new values, think of connecting it with other initiatives and systems, such as compensation, evaluation and assignment of tasks. Many Human Resources professionals struggle for supporting coaching programs as an isolated action; nevertheless they should not do it. In order that coaching attracts a consistent attention with that it seeks, it's needed of the support of the high management and of visible links to the business imperatives.

The best coaches base their work on the environment generated with the individual who's being orientated, through his relations at all levels, plus the values, goals and dynamics of the business of the client. An efficient coach helps someone reach the approved goals, while he transfers the skills and the necessary knowledge to support his constant development. Same as good parents, the good coaches foment independence.

The best coaches perceive the hidden truths. They tend to be onlookers and to formulate penetrating questions. There the aptitude to upturn stones and discover what they conceal turns out to be critical, as business conversations, often, omit essential matters. For instance, one of our clients, president of a medium size and family company contracted some coaching meetings without revealing us that he wanted his son to replace him as president and without divulging us that the other members of the family were convinced that the son was not meeting the compulsory requirements. This set of secret agendas turned out to be much more important than the matters the coaching program had to address. And obviously, the task of unveiling those hidden agendas needs some subtlety.

So, clients' references and testimonies from individuals who have been previously coached are always important for a proper pre-analysis.

Anyway, coaching continues being both an art and a science, ideally practiced by individuals of acute perception, who possess diplomacy, good criterion and, especially, possess the aptitude to manage conflicts with integrity. Probably the most important skills to perform coaching are character and perspective, which come as much from the coach personal experience as from his formal development. Obviously, it's also important to pay attention to the chemistry between coach and coachee.

The potential clients should think about coaching as a way of satisfying the development needs of the employees in order to tackle the tentative problems and expand the growth opportunities. Coaching can help the leaders in transition, for instance those that are evolving from operative positions to staff positions. Here an injection of management coaching can be suitable in order to heighten for instance the managers' self-confidence before moving to that upper level position.

Nevertheless, coaching doesn't seek psychological depth, doesn't pretend to tackle problems such as anxiety or chronic depression, although it is most true that coaching can have the collateral effect of partially "healing" some pathologies, but we must be extremely wary there. It doesn't suit to accept problems that we cannot neither approach nor resolve. When a manager needs this kind of help, it's important to derive that individual to another kind of professionals.

So, once having evaluated his tentative candidate for a coaching process, the clients must make sure that coaching is a process that the chosen prospect really wants to take part in, and where his efforts for changing and growing will be valued and supported by his boss and his colleagues. This support is really what intensifies the benefits of coaching.

The clients have to consider, equally, the specific management benefits that the process can offer. The experienced clients have less probability than the newcomers of investing money in coaching to solve problems of their personnel and, because of it, in general, they prefer concentrating their investments of coaching in their best employees.

This attitude makes sense. For two reasons: individual coaching can be much costlier "per cápita" than many other learning techniques. Secondly, many managers think of a coaching process as a negative badge in their careers. So most clients have to decide if a manager is sufficiently valuable as to justify the cost of coaching.

Another basic thing is the action plan, a living document that gives body and substance to the initially defined goals.

We strongly insist on agreeing SMART measurable goals, which the coachee can realistically reach.

We must select goals that maximize the mutual interests. If the client has a strategic goal and the would-be coachee has a professional goal, for instance, they must identify together a goal that integrates both needs.

The process induces the coaching participants in conceiving terms that produce the specific results they wish. Designing action plans is an iterative and living process that goes along with the new knowledge acquisition.

Obviously, it's always important to be in the disposition of renegotiating the plans months after having being established if one relies on new information that should reveal a path that would produce better results. This adaptability, sometimes, surprises the classical managers used to uniform and "frozen" solutions.

Discuss what has to be discussed and do it with sincerity. Insist on achieving genuine commitments. Identify conflicts and solve them.

In spite of its usefulness for helping an individual or a team, the most profitable coaching strategy consists in developing the whole strata of managers.

Finally, it's important to bear in mind that commitment with coaching implies putting into practice the coaching principles, i.e. working as a coach instead of falling in the temptation of acting as a "classical" manager.

Differences
BETWEEN MANAGER AND COACH

Let's return a few instants to some more general considerations about the environment where the coaching process develops.

We personally use our own model to illustrate the existing ambiguity between manager and coach, between task and attitude, etc...

Let's think of a scale. In a scale, we have 2 plates. The left-side plate represents "the task" (the WHAT), the right side represents "the behavior" (the HOW). Everything we consume in classical management time is focused on "the task". Everything we invest in coaching adds to the "behavior" plate. The key words are "to "spend" and "to "invest" and they have very different implications. The question, and also the problem, takes root in balancing both plates of the scale.

Deeming the manager as a coach and as a creator of a culture for coaching constitutes a new paradigm for the management team. The habitual paradigm, the task, has to do with control, with order and with obedience. This approach has as a consequence that the individuals are considered and treated as a mere commodity. Coaching, on the other hand, pretends to give power to the individuals as those reveal their potential and apply it to the long-term business, the behavior.

Coaching is not a subspecies of management; it is its essential nucleus, at least in a "modern" approach. When managers are really efficient, coaching can signify the real difference between the ordinary manager and the extraordinary one.

The essence of efficient management is empirical enough though.

To presuppose that we can know what generates an appropriate level of results and that we can control all those factors and variables constitute the main barriers to obtaining better results.

The efficient management continues being essentially the art of "achieving things by means of the individuals efforts". Thinking of management as an art, beyond a series of skills, turns out to be potentially more fruitful, as that recognizes it being something more than a mere set of magically revealed skills.

When observing what an efficient manager does, we could conclude that a manager in action looks like somehow an artist.

The managers who pay attention to what happens in their vicinity obtain better results that those who try to apply skills learned by heart, standard recipes and rational models.

The efficiency of the manager arises from the level of association that's created between him and his interlocutors.

Coaching, therefore, as we use the term, refers to the activity of creating, by means of the communication, the climate, the way and the context that gives power, to individuals and to teams, in order to generate outstanding results.

Besides studying what makes a top coach, what can a manager do in order to transform himself into a good coach in the context of his business? What causal actions do produce what specific effects?

What seem to be incontrovertible is that the companies need, nowadays more than ever, individuals who can think by themselves.

Actually, it's a matter of evolving from a paradigm based on hierarchic authority, order and control (besides a motivation based on insecurity) to a paradigm based on cooperation towards the achievement of results and commitment, to collaborating in obtaining new possibilities more than in supporting old structures.

Like it or not, we're tied to a model that tries to control and, more tangibly, to scrutinize the behavior of the employees to improve efficiency, productivity and competitiveness. What's needed in just the contrary.

Coaching captures those essential features in a way that allows the individuals change the paradigm of control / order / prescription into one designed to recognize and give power to the individuals, empowerment. It creates a new context for management, where a genuine association is promoted between managers and employees so that both can achieve more than they had imagined from the perspective of our culture of traditional management.

Because of all the above-mentioned, coaching and empowerment are turning into a strategic need for those companies committed with success.

Though many managers could spontaneously be good coaches, traditionally some fundamental differences exist. Let's see what are those differences.

.

DIFFERENCES

MANAGERS

They are in charge of directing and controlling the results of their people, to obtain predictable results.

They have and are focused on beforehand definite aims

They try to motivate the persons

They are responsible for the persons they direct

They obtain the power through the authority of their position

They centre on what poorly works and why things happen

They look at the future based on predictions

They lead teams

They determine what can do the team

They solve problems bearing in mind the limits and obstacles

They centre on skills in order that the persons do the job

They use rewards and punishments to control behaviors

They are reasonable

They think that the persons work for them

They can like or not the persons who manage

They look for results and can agree, or not, with the reasons why they happen

They support and defend the existing organizational culture

Coaches and leaders

They see their job as a way of "giving power" to the persons in order that they obtain unprecedented results.

They are orientated to the commitments of the persons and align their aims with the common aims of the organization

They insist that the persons are self-motivated

They demand that the persons who undergo a coaching process are self-responsible

They get their power through their relations with the persons who undergo a coaching process and from their mutual commitments

They look at what "is absent"

They look at the future as a possibility

They create possibilities in order that they lead others

They propose novel commitments and then they plan how to realize them

They use limits and obstacles to obtain results without precedents

They provide the persons with a way of examining possibilities and of choosing themselves

They entrust and allow the coachees to decide their own conduct

They are unreasonable

They work for the persons who undergo a coaching process

They look for the results and observe if the actions are consistent with the commitments of the persons

They create a new culture

Kinds of coaches

Now we've seen some differences between managers and coaches, it happens that there are several kinds of coaches.

External Coach:

He is a supplier of the company. It has a particularity: the possession of an external vision or perspective. Besides, here doesn't exist the possibility of initiating power or affective games with the individuals who participate in the coaching process. The variety of his experiences in different companies adds an extra value to his job.

One of the limitations of this modality of coaching is when the coach has not taken part in the determination of the goals and neither is he present during the follow-up or evaluation. All this supposes an important loss of resources, as this kind of coaching can be expensive.

Internal Coach:

We're talking of an employee of the company, subject to its internal rules. His strength rests in knowing thoroughly those rules but his weak point is the very fact of being internal. The coach belongs to the same company that the recipient and, for that reason, possesses the same management culture. In specific occasions, he can have difficulties in helping the coachee acquire perspective in demanding situations, having been confronted to the same restrictions. Another aspect to consider is the relational proximity of the coach with his superiors and with the fellows of the coachee. This situation can hamper real affective neutrality.

Nevertheless, an undoubtedly positive element of internal coaching is its permanency in the long term. Nevertheless, his permanent presence can generate a risk of dependence of the coachee towards him. As we have seen, this dependence turns out to be inconsistent with some of the basic principles of coaching.

The manager coach:

Same as with the internal coach, we talk about someone subject to the rules, culture and political games of the company. Unlike the external coach, the manager coach is a hierarchic superior of his interlocutors. In this respect, it possesses a double role: it centers on the results in the short term, the WHAT, and, at the same time, he is an associate of his development, that's to say, centers on his accompaniment, the HOW. This implies the need not to confuse roles, as his interlocutors can turn out to be tremendously confused by the intervention of this kind of coach.

In this case, the key resides in working first with the manager, in order that he understands coaching as a management skill similar to any another skill and avoiding, thus, tumbling on ambiguities.

These ambiguities are sensitive if the contacts are daily, if the individuals belong to the same team and if the place, physical space, where coaching is performed is in the own office of the manager. It's important to be, so, fully conscious of the limitations of this practice.

Actually, how can a manager coach preserve the necessary neutrality for the good development of a coaching process?

Don't forget that coaching is a learning process.

LEARNING PROCESS IN ADULTS

So, it's possible to say is that, ultimately, coaching is a way of learning for adults.

Until a few years ago, learning and education were developing concepts that automatically made us think about children and teenagers. Nevertheless, children, teenagers and adults, all of us, we constantly learn throughout our whole lifetime. Actually, the obvious differences between adults and children made us think for a long time that learning and education were exclusive of the infants. However, two main differences exist in the learning process of children and adults: the first one is related to the mental maturity and the cognitive processes that facilitate us do inferences beyond the received information. The second one centers on the accumulated experience.

Though we adults have, allegedly, the aptitude to perform this self-evaluation and to decide the best thing for us, we do not always demonstrate this behavior. How many times have we thought that we shouldn't do this or that, but because it forms a part of our routine, we do it?

Coaching is in line with the concepts of adults' learning, however we the adults have the possibility of being critical with our decisions and with our learning process, it doesn't mean that it should necessarily be so. The reasons can be many: routine, laziness, lack of habit, possessing a low self-esteem, etc.

In adults, coaching helps facilitate the learning process. The coach tries to reflect the reality of the coachee, working as a mirror in order that the adult acquires conscience of his reality and can become the owner of his own actions. The individuals who have taken part in some processes of coaching feel that they have the right to decide by themselves and to assume the responsibility for their actions.

Later we're going to penetrate the economic and social context that allows this approach to be accepted. Already we have advanced an important point: if external pressure doesn't exist, nobody rethinks his personal learning models. In other words, nobody steps willfully out of his own comfort zone.

To step out of the comfort zone, we have to be "provoked", and a way very simple to do it's through questions.

Pedagogy of coaching

The methodology based on questions is, because of its nature, the simplest. It drives us back to our childhood. Because of it, the good coach is keen at formulating adequate questions, provoking then the reaction of his coachee.

By the way of deduction, the coachee then comes to his own conclusions and, finally, towards a tacit knowledge, which is the only one that remains anchored in the brain.

The philosophy of this method is, obviously, Socratic and is based on the already mentioned "**Maieutics**".

This approach might be divided into three parts.

1. The first part serves to establish the goals that are to be reached. It is well known that not everybody is equal, and don't even react in the same way; in spite of the fact that the incoming stimuli are identical. Therefore, the process has always to be personalized to every interlocutor. This implies knowing him, empathize with him, establishing a link of communication.

2. The second part has to do with the face-to-face observation, with recommendations and many questions that are directed to trigger the individual's deduction process. This phase normally extends during several months, with a stronger presence in the first months, and slacker later, in order to just confirm the results. The coach is an active beholder who questions, interrogates, but who's abstained from establishing definite conclusions. Often,

he doesn't even provide answers. The coachee that really learns has to identify himself what he does poorly. So the coach, often, doesn't even explore, and only limits himself to observe and highlight facts

3. The third phase is the phase of evaluation and maintenance. It turns out habitual that in a coaching process new personal links appear between the parts, yet having performed it very professionally. The temptation of coming to a coach is always proportional to the interests of permanent improvement from the coachee. Nevertheless, if the lesson has been well learned, the coachee himself, in the future, will do a large part of the work.

Mentoring

Before moving forward, after having spoken about learning models, it is important to clarify an aspect.

Two of the most practiced and known strategies for personal development are coaching and mentoring. Right now, two very fashionable terms and commonly in the mouth of almost all the professionals who integrate our companies. But, do we have an accurate idea of the existing difference between those two models?

Coaching is a process sometimes led by an immediate superior, acting as a coach, who tries to improve the performance of someone at his workplace, with the intention of reaching some shared goals. Sometimes, large companies have a whole team of full-time coaches. Sometimes coaching is led by external individuals.

In some of our clients, large IT companies for instance, both approaches exist in parallel.

Mentoring, on the other hand, is a process by means of which someone with more experience, the mentor, shows, advises, guides and helps with the personal and professional development of his interlocutor, the coachee, or pupil, investing time, energy and knowledge.

The situations where it's required to apply a process of coaching and / or of mentoring are similar enough. The great difference is that while the first one is more adapted to develop already existing skills in the person, mentoring possesses as main goal the grabbing, retention and development of the existing talent inside the company.

But, what are the tangible benefits of mentoring for the company?

People are kept more positive, participative and integrated. It heightens performance, productivity and the motivation of the interlocutors and, consistently, generates a major attraction and retention of the personnel. Besides, we can reduce the cost of training and development because the individuals learn at their own workplace.

A mentoring program, when the process is satisfactory, can be extended to other individuals in the company. As a general rule, the recruitment is often simpler, as that process shows the commitment that the company has with the individuals who integrate it.

In sum, the most common and general benefits for the company that applies a mentoring program are very similar to those of coaching:

- To improve the performance and productivity of the employees.
- To favor the organizational climate.
- To optimize the selection and development of new talents.
- To develop the future leaders.
- To promote static managers.
- To recruit and to retain individuals with high potential and high levels of skills.
- To reduce the turnover of the staff.
- To ameliorate the learning process of the employees, along with the business of the company, its policy, philosophy and "know-how".

Nevertheless, the profile of a mentor is different from a coach's.

Although the classic coach can be a general practitioner, when it comes to talk about mentoring it is obligatory to command some specialty.

The success of the program depends, to a great extent, on the individuals who take part in it. Hence, it, it's necessary to perform a careful selection of the team responsible for the program and also of the participants. As we have already indicated, the mentor is someone who's ready to invest time and energy, to commit with the process and to share his knowledge and his experience. It is advisable, however, that he possesses a preceding positive experience as a mentor or as a coach, a good credibility within the company, some solid interpersonal skills and a genuine interest in the individuals' development.

Identifying a suitable mentor is not an easy task, as it will require from him to invest some time and effort. To carry out this search, it's not compulsory to centre only on the top staff of the company, but on the whole staff and on who's willing to help people and collaborate in new projects.

Everybody within the company can benefit from a mentoring program. The most advisable thing is to administer a questionnaire in order that all those individuals of the company who want to be coachees complete it. The election of the coachee will change depending on the criteria of the company.

To obtain success in a process of mentoring, the figure of the coordinator turns out to be vital. The coordinator's role in a mentoring program is to support the strategy and the goals of the process, both of the participants and of the company. Obviously, the coordinator has to rely on his knowledge of the company and on some excellent interpersonal skills. His function rests in avoiding the problems that could arise between mentor and coachee and, should those take place, be rapid in his management and resolution of the situation and in the insurance that such a situation disappears. His main assignments consist in helping with the selection, evaluation, fitting in and orientation of the mentors and of the coachees.

However, it is by no means incompatible to include a part of mentoring inside a coaching process, if we determine that the coachee needs the development of a special skill in order to be able going forward. Simply, this part has to be distinctly differentiated.

Virtual Coaching

A variant or complement is the so-called virtual coaching. The virtual coaching is the application of coaching face to face, albeit through new technologies, by means of the use of multimedia environments that allows interactivity, confidentiality, analysis, reflection, confidence and support of the relation between coach and coachee.

Obviously, we're talking about something much wider that the kind of help we could give our interlocutor using simply e-mail, or from a web workgroup.

It can be something complementary to a face-to-face coaching process, but we must be firmly sure that it doesn't replace it.

Some of its advantages are:

- It allows the coachee improve his performance at his own pace.
- It's individualized training.
- It facilitates new readings and perceptions.
- It allows a major confidentiality.
- It allows overcome the barriers of time and distance.
- It reduces the costs of coaching.
- It opens new possibilities towards the coachees: in different hierarchic levels, separated from the management positions.
- It allows working on behavioral and emotional issues more easily.

- It facilitates the analysis and the reflection.
- It allows a major agility in the process.

Let's stress, once again, that this kind of coaching doesn't replace "physical" coaching.

2 - The environment

Think of the parable of the frog in the pot. Remember: If you pick a pot, fill it with cold water and gently put a living frog in the pot; without putting the lid on, and them put the pot on the kitchen fire and start heating the water, what will happen, believe it or not, is that the frog will eventually die. The frog, because the increase of temperature is constant and gradual, doesn't perceive that constant increase until the water is too hot, not necessarily boiling, and its metabolism eventually collapses.

On the other hand, if we previously heat the water and repeat the procedure, then the frog will instantly leap out of the pot.

The same appears with change. Change is constant, but sometimes we are not fully aware of it, and once we realize the water is hot, it is generally too late.

However, what sometimes happens is a totally unexpected crisis that allows countries, companies or even individual realize some major change in their behaviors. True, crisis might be traumatic, but they also are a poke in the ribs, a reason for leaping out and not dying a slow and painful death.

This metaphor connects with the reason why we must shift some management paradigms, in particular applying tools like coaching, instead of clinging to classical approaches.

CHANGE

As we have previously and profusely commented on, coaching consists of a process, a process that allows us face a changing environment. If change wouldn't exist, there would be no need for coaching. But we know that the environment changes at an unstoppable and increasing pace.

We're trying to underline that coaching and change are two entwined words. Coaching will generate an internal change in ourselves, who will allow us fight the external change, the heating water.

Nevertheless, normally change is not something agreeable. Besides, change also constitutes a process, never to be treated as an isolated fact. Everybody has to walk through four different phases when it comes to facing it:

1 - Denial.

When change takes place, the first reaction is of immediate denial. "Who came up with that stupid idea?" "It will never work here". This attitude is similar to the ostrich', hiding its head in the sand, hoping that change will pass by and won't affect us.

We lived an interesting situation many years ago in a meeting with a group of managers. We told them that the Japanese companies were at war with the western companies and that we had to prepare ourselves for what was on its way. One of the managers spontaneously and angrily protested. His exact words were: *"Fine by me, but I am not at war with anybody. I am not willing to enter a fight with the Japanese"*. Needless to say, although it took a few years to occur, eventually his company went bankrupt.

So we can deny change, but change will inevitably happen, whether we like it or not.

2 - Resistance.

At some moment, you eventually notice that change is there. Nevertheless, this acceptance doesn't mean that you have to live through change without moving a finger.

"I will continue doing my work as always. If this system has worked until now, it will continue so". Resistance is a perfectly normal reaction opposite to change; the whole world experiences it. The key resides in not allowing resistance to generate stagnation. The sooner the program starts, the better it will be for the company and the better it will be for you.

3 - Exploration.

Come to this point, you already know that there's no point in resisting and that the new way of doing the things can have even its advantages.

"Hummm... well, probably this change makes sense. I will see what opportunities will allow me take some advantage of change". During this exploration stage, you examine the good things and the bad derivatives of change and choose your strategy for dealing with it.

4 - Acceptance.

The last stage of change is acceptance. Come to this point, you will have managed to integrate change in your daily routine. "Cheers, this new system really works very well. It doesn't bear any point of comparison with the way we were doing things before". Now the change that you initially refused and to which you resisted with such a strong vehemence, is a part of your daily routine; and then change has turned into a new "status quo".

After having gone through all these reactions before change, the circle is closed and you are now ready for the next challenge.

Our somewhat protectionist economy, in our western culture, has focused on the management of the Doing, the WHAT, where the individuals do their best in order to perform a given task, always avoiding trying anything different without requesting the mandatory permission.

That way, before the appearance of problems, the individuals don't face and solve them on their own but they expose the matter or the complaint to their boss and ultimately ask him: *"Boss, what do I do?"* In this situation, the boss thinks for his interlocutor and communicates him clearly, or not, what he has to do.

The management of the Being, the HOW, is the response for administering the new paradigms.

The management of the Doing, the WHAT, has led us to conceive individuals as a basic resource of the company leveled to capital, technology and information. We identify the individuals as mere human resources, expecting them to do only what's programmed, denying them the right to think by themselves. That way, in many companies an un-human culture has developed, where the interlocutors are not like they look, but as the boss hopes them to be.

In that culture, the employee only does that he is told to do and doesn't go beyond that. And eventually the company pays a very high price for it.

"Modern" managers, on the other hand, recognize and value the contribution the interlocutors can make and try to stimulate and generate the propitious environment so their creative talents can be used in the benefit of them all. No doubt, at all the company levels we can produce creative thinking. The good ideas that contribute to improving the company results arise in any team or person, from a workshop operator to the president of the company. Those ideas must be evaluated and put into practice when they truly deserve it.

Creativity is simply the most intense way of thinking by means of which, with the elimination of the barriers or mental blockades, new alternatives of solution are suggested.

Because of it, in order to face the challenges tossed at us by our contemporary world, we need managers who can actually combine rational and logical thinking with creative vision and intuitive reason. Hence, the commanding trend in education must evolve from analytical reasoning, with an almost total exclusion of intuitive reasoning, towards intuition and development of creative thinking.

Besides, the creative process becomes more productive with the use of checklists, appraisal of the value of the ideas, request and interchange of ideas, sponsorship of the diversity of interests and satisfaction of the individual needs. Routine and tedious operations, where there's a minimal participation of the mind, prevent creativity from blossoming.

And without creativity, we can feel helpless in front of the permanent change.

CHANGE AND NEW SKILLS

Let's think for a moment about all of those changes that happened in the management environment in the last decades. It's true that they are innumerable, but what have the companies done in order to survive and grow in that turbulent environment?

The main response could be: seeking to promote their internal assets. The most classic, likely and easy approach consists of concentrating on economic or financial assets or, maybe, towards technology, although not changing anything in depth. But, does this orientation really guarantee a competitive edge? We reckon that refusing change probably is not a good solution, although we understand how hard fully embracing may be, simply because the above-mentioned change demands that first WE change. And only through that personal change will we be able to deal with the external change.

In this changeable environment, the value of a company doesn't reside, not only, in his tangible and / or technological assets. As already mentioned and strongly stressed, in the traditional management industrial practice, physical assets are considered to be the basis of the company success and wealth. Hence, it is most avoided, sometimes in an involuntary way, to resort to other kinds of assets, which are not at that time estimated at their real and utmost importance.

This, nowadays, is far from true. It's important to centre on the scientific, technical and specialized knowledge, on experience, on skills, and on the individuals capacities and potentials. Hence, there are more and more companies that are growing on the basis of what they can do and not on what they produce.

Nowadays, such assets as patents, licenses, products, services, "know how ", organizational capacities and productive strengths are based on capacities of permanent innovation related to the application of knowledge.

A company capable of discovering and administering those capacities will have a competitive advantage when time comes to translate this intellectual capital into financial and sustainable profitable capital. Nevertheless, in order that the knowledge turns into a source of competitive advantage, it's not sufficient to acknowledge its mere existence. Also it's important to grab this knowledge, distribute it, store it, share it and use it. We're talking here about knowledge management.

Classically, have been identified, in the management context, at least, three dimensions for knowledge.

1. On one hand, the capital is defined as the value generated thanks to the interchange of information with external managers like, for instance, clients and suppliers.

2. It's possible, also, to recognize the structural capital as the value of the knowledge generated in the company and that we translate in an aptitude to be productive. However, all of that is determined, among other aspects, by the organizational culture, the procedures, the processes, the brands, the technological developments, etc.

3. The third dimension contributes to the intellectual capital or the value of the knowledge created by the individuals who integrate the company, their potentials, learning capacity, skills, personal development, experience, etc.

In times characterized by constant flows of information and by changes, an accurate exigency is that companies constantly restate their interactions with the environment and look for strategic differences. That way, they generate new knowledge by means of experience and learning, after having identified and qualified the new sources of knowledge and are provided with the aptitude to correctly administer them.

And so, the development of a company that's based on knowledge turns out to be possible, which is characterized by its aptitude to catch, analyze, distribute and manage the internal information and to transform it into knowledge that adds value to everything what it does. Obviously, this turns out to be totally impossible in a company where the goals don't contemplate the personal and professional development of its employees and where the consideration of the constant search of the utilization of the potential of the innovation is, at best, despised.

Let's examine then, what are the tracks to be explored.

DEVELOPING THE POTENTIAL

Empowerment means creating an environment where the employees feel that they have a real influence on the standards of quality, service and efficiency of the business inside their areas of responsibility. This perception generates a commitment from the employees that makes possible for them reach the goals of the company with a sense of commitment and of self-control. On the other hand, this model also implies that the managers are ready to resign part of their authority and to surrender it to their reports and their teams.

A CLASSIC FORMULA

Motivation is POWER vs RESPONSIBILITY
    If power is higher than responsibility, the result will lead to an autocratic conduct of the individual.

If responsibility is higher than power, the result leads to the frustration of the employees, as they lack the necessary power to assume the activities for which they are responsible.

If both parameters are properly balanced and adjusted, we will have a situation like this:

- The employees feel responsible not only for their task, but for helping the company work better.
- The individual transforms himself into an active agent of solution of his problems.
- The employee takes decisions instead of being a simple recipient of orders.
- The companies are designed to facilitate the tasks of its employees.

But all of this is not, by any means, a natural process. It must be inserted into a wider perspective.

LEARNING, CHANGE AND CULTURE

So, what does happen if we don't integrate coaching into our model of change?

Usually the following thing can happen. The rates of management mortality are high, but management suicides are rare. What are the reasons for those deaths? In some sectors, the response is obvious: the companies die because the environment changes when they don't. Nevertheless, the specific thing is that the environment changes for everybody. This situation alludes to the parable of the frog in the pot. The frog, because the increase of temperature is constant and gradual, doesn't perceive that constant increase until the water is too hot and its metabolism collapses.

Well, the same applies both to human beings and companies.

When the "know-how" of a company, its products offer and its labor relations are in harmony with the environment, the task of the management teams revolves into a mere assignment of resources. The human and financial resources will be assigned to those parts of the company best placed for extracting the highest profit from a stable environment. However, when the environment is unstable, the policy of growth must be substituted by a policy of survival.

Sometimes, a change in policy fails in yielding all the expected results. True to be said, in the excitement caused by permanent expansion, it is rather demanding to adequately perceive changes in the environment or, more perilously, to contemplate them as what they are not. Besides, in a period of prosperity, the part of the company that once benefited the most from the "status quo" situation has become more powerful and independent. The companies insist too much on those policies that during long periods of time produced good results, and then, all of a sudden, without realizing it, they enter a major crisis, and realize that their structures, their systems and people are not ready to face the new challenges. The key question is then: Why don't companies perceive the tell tale signs of incoming change?

It's a question for which it is important to find a response. Human nature fiercely resists to change, which, at first glance, is good, otherwise we would live in a constant chaos. Nevertheless, when change is a requisite for survival, it's compulsory to overcome the natural resistance. And the way of doing it uses to be painful.

In situations of crisis, the deeper the same, the less time and options to face it. And, nevertheless the long-lived companies tell us that it's possible to perceive the signs of change before it happens. So, why do so many of them fail in seeing what happens around them?

It seems that a part of the brain is constantly busy making plans and programs for the future. Those plans are organized in a sequential way; that's to say, they constitute temporary routes towards the future. The healthier and more creative the brain is, the more numerous temporary routes it develops. And, somewhat surprising as it may seem, the brain also stores the alternate routes.

Through our sensory organs, a lot of information enters the brain and a lot of the same must be ignored in order for the organ to adequately work, otherwise, we would be running overdrive and confused by the sheer amount of data flowing through brain. Nevertheless, if a correspondence takes place between the new information and one of the temporary alternate stored routes, we don't ignore the information, and so we can perceive its meaning. This situation interests very much the coach, because that is precisely the entry route to the coachee's brain.

The message is clear: we will perceive the signs proceeding from the outside world only if they turn out to be relevant for some option of future that we have already drafted.

Intelligence transformer is a learning process that examines and evolves from the current suppositions under which operates the company and then develops new organizational practices based on new suppositions.

To embody the intelligence transformer, we need to rely on something more than knowledge and new comprehension. The new knowledge has to lodge itself in the tacit organizational practices until it turns out into routine. However, as a first step, let's remember that the abandon of routine, is one of the bases of experiential learning.

We begun with the question of why some companies assume first some revolutionary ideas, such as power and responsibility given to the employees, total quality, leadership with vision of future, reengineering, information technology, whatever … then start shock treatments to put them into practice; and, after some time, come to the conclusion that those ideas don't work.

The reason is that in many occasions, the individuals have dealt with but not integrated those changes.

Basically, this happens for two reasons:

First

Hitherto has proliferated the most conservative model, called the model of "control and then control". The companies have been capable of efficiently working with just some classical conceptions about human nature and have grown under the supposition that hierarchy is a compulsory and sufficient of control and coordination mechanism.

For that very reason, usually companies are seeking and contracting managers instead of leaders and coaches.

The underlying reason is that the companies have been capable of working under the above-mentioned suppositions in reasonably predictable and stable environments, in markets that were changing at a slow pace, with technologies that they were slowly evolving; and, why not, in molasses political-economic environments that were allowing success, even with relatively low levels of efficiency.

Nevertheless, nowadays, we have already spoken about it, the environment changes at a very high pace. The same thing happens with technologies and markets, and globalization demands us to compete with companies that are much more productive and efficient. The need to change is today much higher than twenty or thirty years ago, we will never stress it enough. Nevertheless, when we observe the results immediately after some attempts of transformation, we meet few companies that have managed to deal in a suitable way with the above-mentioned changes.

Second

The second reason takes root in the companies' cultures and even in the national cultures where companies are immersed. And the fact is that cultures evolve very slowly and, except when some big crises take place, they skimp the required fundamental cultural changes. Obviously, we refer to real cultural changes, not to programs that are tagged as of "creation of new culture", which in general use to be mere alibis, and don't change anything; although they sound pretty fashionable.

If the changes we want to implement appear to question the basic suppositions of the company, they usually meet resistance or incomprehension. In other words, the second reason that explains why the organizational transformations are so scanty is that they demand us to abandon some deep cultural paradigms and rebuild the company on new ones. And this kind of "de-learning" and posterior learning is, necessarily, slow and painful.

So, how can we improve the learning process? What are the conditions, necessary and sufficient, for "un-learn" and for re-learn? To analyze this question, it's compulsory to check some of the psychological dynamics linked to anxiety. It is known that when our former models stop working, we experience confusion. We enter a state of disquiet that we can name "disquiet of survival". Unless we change, we won't reach our goals, and, in some extreme cases, won't even survive.

Nevertheless, disquiet generates in us the perspective to abandon some of our suppositions and tacit practices. It's the uneasiness of learning.

The stronger the uneasiness we experience, the stronger vehemence we will put into rejecting the new information and the more adamantly we will stick to our already known systems. This process is named "resistance to change" and, undoubtedly, it's something natural and predictable. As a consequence, in order that change takes place it's compulsory that the survival anxiety overcomes the learning one.

The problem is that, often, generating the sufficient psychological safety in order to overcome the anxiety produced by a learning process is very demanding. Especially when, simultaneously, significant increases in productivity are demanded. Undoubtedly, such psychological safety is totally absent when companies are immersed in staff reduction processes or in reorganization towards a leaner structure. Actually, in order to feel psychologically safe we need some time and space to think, allowing time for the information to settle in our brain. We need some training for learning how to learn.

In that context, coaching emerges again as a powerful option, as the coach can help generate, undoubtedly, a sufficient level of psychological safety.

"Selfish" Coaching

As we have already commented, in order that a coaching process works, i.e., that it finally ends up modifying a behavior, several preceding stages exist, in order to connect with the motivations of the coachees.

A very different thing is to try to project my, as a coach, or as a manager, personal motivations onto my coachees.

The labor life of a manager affects his life quality, in the form of negative emotions, physical and psychic fatigue and also nervous tension, downright visible or merely underlying.

All of this, besides, exercises a tremendous influence on the personal life. And precisely all of those elements, negative emotions, fatigue, tension, etc., arise amongst those who, mostly, hamper the efficiency or the performance of the personnel management.

It's important to tackle this kind of curse and generate another circle, a virtuous circle, where self-accomplishment and satisfaction for achievement nourish the intrinsic motivation and the personal performance.

When it becomes unavoidable, a good coach can help us neutralize what's negative in our surroundings, but also he can help us exploit what's positive.

Pretty often nowadays, in some big companies, a function assigned to the boss is coaching, especially with young interlocutors with a promising future. This practice is not necessarily efficient. As we have beheld, being a boss and practicing coaching is not actually the same thing.

The coach must help the coachee adopt the most beneficial attitudes and find his own answers before questions that probably had not been previously formulated. We, as many other individuals, need a kind of personal reengineering and here, undoubtedly, a good coach can help us.

It's not a matter, of course, of giving him advice, but of extracting the best from the coachee; of making him come to the best conclusions in the best ways. And, if we can improve in efficiency, even more can we improve in life, which besides concerns our job environment and also, obviously, our closest personal environment.

THE JOB ENVIRONMENT OF THE MANAGERS

We talk about labor climate, which relates to the professional satisfaction; and not only about pursuing a career or simply earning money.

Nevertheless, those postulates are perfectly compatible with the focus on the task; although it is most true that some of the powerful slogans that circulate in the companies are, often, poorly understood. For instance: quality, empowerment, teamwork, learning...

Anyway, if we perform the effort to live "here and now", we can enjoy the daily activity and reach a high performance. That happens when the task, although challenging our capacity, stimulates us sufficiently.

Definitively, we can be perfectly comfortable writing a report, visiting a client, solving a problem, assigning tasks, preparing a catalogue or an offer, lecturing a conference, installing electronic equipment, looking for information in Internet, designing a program or acquiring new knowledge.

It happens when:
- We face challenges that we can assume.

- We are absolutely concentrated on the activity.
- There are clear goals to reach.
- The activity gives us feedback immediately.
- It seems to us that we're overcoming the challenge with surprising facility.
- We don't care about the risks or of the dangers that the activity implies.
- We lose the notion of ourselves.
- The sense of duration is altered.
- The activity comes to constitute a purpose in itself.
- We feel a specific intimate elation of victory.

The coach, obviously, can help us heighten the above-mentioned conditions that, as we know, contribute both to professional efficiency and to satisfaction and enjoyment. All of them, actually, feed the improvement of efficiency, thanks to a real connection with the motivation of the employee.

However, if there something else that we can do before becoming a coach? The response is affirmative. It would be fine to begin, first, by increasing our self-knowledge and by promoting our self-criticism; at least, we can try to start walking that path.

If we were falling into self-deception, probably only an excellent coach might save us.

Let's remember some features of the managers who self-deceive themselves:

- Arrogance.
- Thirst of power.
- Excessive worship of the ego.
- Obsession to appear perfect.
- Jactitation.
- Disability to admit mistakes or critiques.
- Narcissism.
- Pursuit of poorly realistic goals.

Precautions

In order not to deceive us, there are some precautions to be taken.

Undoubtedly, it's of great help to rely on computer systems that allow us construct information. But little usefulness they will offer us if we're not capable of managing "face to face" meetings that allow us working with individuals.

It's important to say that "face to face" is extrapolable to groups. Then it's simply named group coaching.

Traditionally, the weakest facet of the manager has always been skills management and motivation of his interlocutors. It looks like a paradox, but often the good technical preparation contrasts with the lack of skills related to them. This situation has propitiated the continuity of autocratic models or other styles that are distinctly incompatible with the development of the intellectual capital in a modern company.

The personalized coaching meetings approach development situations of the potential of the manager. The most habitual reasons of intervention use to be: decisions making, conflicts, stress management, search for resources, development of specific skills, support of promotions, etc.

Giving a tangible example, the coaching meetings for groups have as a goal to stir into action a group of individuals or managers. The most habitual interventions use to be: problem solving, creativity meetings, resolution of conflicts, etc.

Finally, the sessions of training in coaching allow the participants develop their skills as coaches in order that they can stimulate the potential of their interlocutors and, that way, improve their performance.

Those interventions can be formal when a specific frame is established, but also informal when the coach takes advantage of the opportunities of on-the-job challenges to put into practice the model. Also we can use the methodology for our own development (self coaching).

WHAT'S THE ESSENCE OF THE MODEL?

Our results are a consequence of our actions and behaviors and those, in turn, are the reflex of our thoughts. The performance improvement takes place when we enrich our mental models and are in disposition, afterwards, to generate new answers.

In any case, the essence of coaching always looks for the mental model of the coachee to develop, increasing his level of conscience and facilitating him to move towards action. All this process is performed through questions and is supported by descriptive and not evaluative feedback.

The sequence might be, inspired on the G.R.O.W. (Goal, Reality, Options, Will) model for instance

1. Description of the wished situation (goal)
2. Description of the current situation (area of improvement or difficulty)
3. Map of options and of resources (generation and selection)
4. Action plan (specific performance plan)
5. Results (control and follow-up)

Here, as you have noticed, we assume that the "Will" is already there.

In the first and second phase, the goal of the coach is to heighten the level of conscience, sensory and emotional, of the coachee. Those initial phases are fundamental, as we can control only one what we are really conscious of. Acquiring conscience gives us the power to act.

In the third phase, the goal is to involve the coachee in the generation of alternatives and in the creation of a personal action plan. Finally, we determine how and when we're going to evaluate the results.

The interactivity of the coach with the coachees confirms his personal aptitude to "opening doors and windows" in people. It generates the sufficient restlessness, always through "precise questions" more than of "accurate affirmations", as to awake in others the same "thirst" that he possesses himself.

And all of that, always bearing in mind the specificities of every company, consequently adapting the strategy to each situation and to different cultural values.

Cultural values

We act in agreement to our cultural values because the relations in the long term with our suppliers and our clients matter for us. At least, this is the way it should be.

It's necessary to outline the behaviors that are expected from the individuals in a given situation.

Again, here we talk of the HOW, as a stage prior to obtaining the significant WHAT.

With a few specific adjustments, we can use the following tools.

Preceding analysis

When it comes to measuring the cultural values, there's no room for surprises. The companies have to accurately describe to their employees what to correctly perform their tasks means and to explain in detail and in writing all the compulsory and foreseen actions and behaviors. All this has to remain perfectly clear and, besides, it must be unique and accessible to all.

The employees not only have to understand those behaviors but they must harbor the certainty that their supervisors evaluate them adequately according to those behaviors. The details have to remain distinctly definite and the individuals have to know perfectly what they are doing.

The supervisors evaluate the coachees according to their own observations: they observe and determine if the behaviors, as the company has defined them, are consistent with the corporate values. Such observations are quantified using a scale of evaluation of the behavior. The scale describes the wished behaviors and evaluates the personnel depending on four criteria:

> 0 - no evidence,
> 1 - efficient,
> 2 - very efficient and
> 3 - exceptional.

360° EVALUATION

The 360° evaluation process is another management tool available to human resources. This process allows the managers to be evaluated about practically everything by those individuals with whom they are in contact, employees, own fellows, superiors, even clients. Beware though; it properly works only if it actually measures behaviors that add a real value.

The essential conclusion that can be extracted from the survey is that the 360° evaluation is never convenient to be used alone. It must never constitute the only information in the Development Plan of the coachees. The most suitable utilization of the tool is as a support for the coachees so it is easier to understand where they must improve their behavior, based on the commentaries of the people. It has to be combined with a self-evaluation to determine how the evaluated ones feel about their work, in comparison with how the people see it.

Both approaches serve to identify and to address the weak points. The coachees can work with their bosses in order to generate an analysis of the deficiencies, comparing the individual performance with the obligatory behavior skills to be used at their workplace. The results are then attached to the periodical appraisal of the employee.

Quite sensibly, both 360° evaluation and self-analysis work better if a coaching process focused on behaviors is later performed.

Supporting behaviors

Most companies fail when it comes to reinforcing the correct behaviors. In general, we work with the employees according to the standard educational philosophy that says "study, try, study". When the goal is to teach new behaviors, this approach doesn't ensure full results. Learning to drive a truck has nothing to do with inspiring people. Working on attitudes and working on aptitudes are different things altogether.

The best programs of behavioral development are based on a philosophy of "learning by doing" and skills extracted from experiential learning (see "The paper bridge"). We talk of a process of constant development in the person that devotes time to absorb, fix and apply the learned skills to his daily work. The last goal is to develop participative and flexible employees, capable of rapidly adapting as changes become more and more demanding.

The role of the leaders

When it comes to implementing some cultural values, the importance of the top management must not be underestimated. The current studies reveal that the top management, and not only the direct supervisors, is evolving into a key component for the satisfaction of the employees. The top managers must send an accurate message about how the cultural values help reach the goals and fulfill the mission of the company. Besides, they must live in agreement with such values in order that the employees understand better what the wished behaviors mean in practice.

Finally, it would be convenient if the leaders were periodically checking the essential values of the company to, verify that these continue being applied. This action is of special relevancy in the global companies that are compelled to consider the social expectations when it comes to defining the corporate cultures. For instance, it's fair to surmise that the leaders of many business units who operate in Europe will have a series of expectations different from those of his American counterparts.

In this context, obviously, the management of Human resources requires some nuances to be introduced.

Management of human resources

Traditionally, Human resources management has always been related to the administration of whatever has to deal with the company employees in a functional and operational way.

What it should have to do, nevertheless, is starting with the consumer instead of with the producer (pull instead of push).

Actually, modern times demand new social models, where what's important is to be efficient but not only in an individual way. This approach is possible only with a labor coordinated with the whole group.

The sense and the "raison d'être" of the management policy of human development consists of orientating the potential of knowledge, of the company intelligence, of the values and of the communication, with the final intention of delivering quality services to the clients; always due to the fact that the market has changed.

Though many companies have been successful so far, even coming from a traditional protectionist system, such a situation turns out to be obsolete in a opened, where the quality processes constitute a first rank exigency to guarantee competitive prices and services to the market.

Because of its nature, the human resources management needs to integrate a dynamic company vision, in order to be able to meet the demand of its personnel in the different facets that affect the company management and on which depends, to a great extent, the response that this same gives to its clients.

In this quest for production and quality systems more environment-sensitive, the treatment of the individuals must lead us to a new reflection, to a dynamics of the productive structure based on a novel management of human resources.

The traditional factors of production like land (natural resources), work and capital are now secondary. They have been replaced by information and knowledge.

If we examine the history of society, three changes, three fundamental transformations have taken place: the industrial revolution, the productivity revolution and the administrative revolution, in which we are currently immersed. Today, more information than products are interchanged.

Nevertheless, the culture of the companies are not prepared to assimilate the above-mentioned change, which implies that without quality individuals quality processes don't exist.

Therefore, the organizational structures, both processes and systems, must be beheld from another vantage point: the point of improvement and adaptability to the new society and to the customer-oriented culture.

The human brain has unlimited possibilities of modifying paradigms. It can adjust and adapt and it is perfectly capable of integrating new paradigms and forgetting former conflicts. Everything that comes to dislocate the former established order in our life is a potential triggering for transformation, for putting us in movement towards a major maturity, towards an opening and a heightened power.

Besides, the motivation is, mainly, interior, intrinsic. It's a question of the power that can remain asleep for a lot of time; in fact, in some individuals it can remain passively buried the whole life without ever managing to show out.

If motivation were external, anyone who, for instance, attends a personal motivation training session would walk out motivated in equal degree and in equal intensity. And it turns out that actually, some walk out of those trainings prepared to completely change their anterior point of view. However, with the passing of days their enthusiasm abates and they return to their habitual way of life. Others, they choose to modify their life; and their progress is, to all accounts, obvious. Meanwhile, other individuals will only comment that the topic was very interesting, but they still have to consider putting into practice some of the exposed concepts.

If someone depends on other individuals to act, probably he will not get the most out of his life. It's like that, because he is not using his interior motivation that, ultimately, is the only motive power that leads to success. Practical examples of such individuals' typology abound in all kinds of companies. They are individuals who don't want to perform a better job because they don't feel motivated by their bosses and, due to their attitude, are frequently forgotten when it comes to promotion. Those individuals live always seeking their great motivator as if it was a question of a Messiah or of a miraculous elixir.

Dread, obviously, also constitutes a great motivator, but the results probably won't last. The behaviors provoked by fear are not lasting long, unless some positive motivator reinforces them. As an example, we can think of, let's say, putting our seat belt on when driving; in order to be integrated, that behavior requires the fear of being fined mixed with the prospect of saving lives, mine included by the way.

When someone works influenced by the threat of dismissal, he can neither have the compulsory concentration, obviously, nor be in good disposition to walk some additional step to make his work better. As it seems to be logical, he will only do the compulsory thing to please his bosses. And only that.

The best existing motivator is desire; the almost compulsive need to obtain success in life. To aspire to climb the mountain and plant our flag on the top. This is the motivation trigger that really functions. And this motivation only exists inside each of us. It's something like a compressed spring, with all his energy ready to be released. Everything we have to do is press the button. Obviously easier said than done.

Often, nevertheless, many people procrastinate, and when they eventually perform, they have run out of time.

The best employee a company can have is the one that can be self-motivated. A self-motivated employee works for himself and, therefore, he himself must be congratulated for his achievements.

We have not to be surprised, therefore, that the self-motivated individuals tend to occupy the most relevant positions in any company. It's not by sheer luck that, as an employee ascends the hierarchic ladder, he receives less praise whenever it carries out a good work. Firstly, because the company expects him to always perform well and secondly because his interior motivation should be bigger, because obtaining victories heightens our desire to continue forward and to obtain more successes.

This way, it seems to be clear that constraint or dread don't constitute good "strings" to pull.

SUITABLE MOTIVATIONAL TRIGGERS

In the classic paradigm, the regulation mechanism is control, and control is essentially sustained in dread, in the dread of the consequences for the possible breach. This strategy has supported the labor relations in many companies. But it's not, at least no longer, the best solution...

Fear could have been efficient, in some occasions, to achieve an individual task, the WHAT, but it's not a great method for promoting the coordination activities that ensure the functioning of a group of individuals as a team. For that, we must work on constant learning, the HOW.

The new mechanisms need to rely on a different strategy. They need to generate confidence. It corresponds to the management to specify the challenges and the general goals to reach, in a permanent dialogue with who has the skills for the generation of business possibilities and opportunities.

To obtain such an effect, the management would have to allow their employees some significant spaces of responsible autonomy, allowing them to perform that work of reflection and learning, many times through a coaching process.

All this is built, we insist, on the basis of confidence. It's not only a matter of words. Perhaps some companies don't have in their employees very strong followers; however, employees and companies have, often, interests that can be common.

They consider the individual from the plurality of motives related, for instance, to the top levels of Maslow's pyramid or to the motivator factors of Herzberg. In this book, as we already stated it, we won't go back to the basis of motivational theories, so let's take a shortcut to some partial elements of the same.

The perception of an interest in the remuneration system represents the second hope: that of being rewarded if the awaited results are achieved.

The individual feels attracted by the kind of remuneration, where the expectation coincides with the remuneration supplied by the company.

Besides, he insists on the subtle and delicate balance between expectations and remuneration, what's not always, to put it mildly, always easy to achieve.

The individual holds the co-responsibility for developing his attitudes, in order that the new aptitudes, the skills, can be integrated.

And, at this point, after having spoken about attitude and about aptitude, it's compulsory to comment on some aspects.

As we must not forget that a coaching process will force us work on aptitudes, what's quite easy, but also and especially on attitude: "*do I really want to change something in my current behavior?*"

ATTITUDE AND APTITUDE

The debate between attitude and aptitude or skills is very common in the organizational bibliography.

The skills, thinking of them as habitual behaviors, are the result of a mix of innate characteristics, knowledge and attitudes of the person. The innate characteristics are those genetic aspects that concern behaviors. When we talk about skills development, it's important to concentrate on knowledge development, and on attitudes.

Knowledge is obtained through the acquisition of new information. In other words, of quantitative and qualitative information about reality.

That way, prior to developing any kind of skill, e.g., negotiation, teamwork or time management, it's suitable to begin with acquiring some theoretical knowledge on the topic.

Nevertheless, the transmission of knowledge is not an automatic process. To actually incorporate the new information into the already existing one, clarity of approach is needed on the part of the issuer, as well as a suitable and, obviously, a specific degree of mental opening and of intellectual effort on the part of the recipient.

And here starts the really demanding stuff, as working on attitudes turns out to be much more complicated that working on aptitudes. At first, few individuals show a positive predisposition to modifying their attitudes.

The attitudes are those motivations that someone possesses towards action. The development of the appropriate attitudes needs of a training process that qualifies the individual to anticipate the consequences of his actions and of his omissions. Thus, the aptitude for assessing reality acquires a major importance.

As a consequence, the individual can have new motives for the action. For instance, someone who possesses theoretical knowledge on how to work in team is not necessarily willing to work in a team.

But, ultimately, only if this individual really wants to work in a team, will he be capable of developing that skill. The same applies to any other skill.

Skills can be defined as those operative capacities that facilitate action. Skills development needs of a training process. New habits and different manners of acting are acquired through repetition.

So far, so good; problem is, knowledge, attitudes and skills don't develop in an isolated way. They interact dynamically during the skills training depending on the innate characteristics of each person.

In that model, the process of decision that leads to action begins with two kinds of knowledge: the abstract one and the experimental one. The first one includes the theoretical information and the information to which we have referred above, such as knowledge. The second one comes from the experience (from experiences and from experiments).

Experimental knowledge generates a spontaneous motivation towards action. The attitude opposite to action can come from a spontaneous or rational motivation. The rational motivation appears when the individual, exercising his own will, uses his knowledge to anticipate the possible consequences of the action. The rational motivation leads us to act according to the convenience of the action.

Virtuality is that habit that allows us decide based on some rational motivation; i.e., according to what it's important to do and not according to what's more attractive. In order that the decision transforms into action, are needed the operative corresponding skills. Finally, as a consequence of the action, the operative skills develop and new experimental knowledge takes place.

This process can be applied to any skill. For instance, in the case of coaching, a manager who doesn't have this skill might start first learning about it. There, the manager would receive information on the topic and would extend the content of his abstract knowledge. Nevertheless, provided that up to that moment he has not practiced yet, his experience will incline him not to use coaching and, for that very reason, his attitude before it might be of rejection. In consequence, it is most likely that the training program turns out to be insufficient to modify his habits with regard to that particular skill.

Along with this example, the manager should begin by giving example when putting into practice this skill. Simultaneously, that should help him think about the advantages that this way of acting can have both for him and for his people.

Undoubtedly, a compulsory element for the development of any skill is the will, to want, of the manager for putting into practice what he has discovered through information and external training. That will, which comes from personal freedom, possesses two slopes: the rationality for wanting to use the information and the virtuality to do what's more suitable, although at that precise moment it wouldn't turn out to be the most attractive thing to do.

In our example of a manager who's immersed in a process of developing his coaching skill, first he must want to use the new information learned about coaching and, later, he must be capable of adopting the decisions to apply it in each specific case.

For instance, the manager can have learned that in order to do coaching it's necessary to assume that the coachee might commit some mistake.

Provided that the operative skills develop with every action, the posterior action will be more efficient and will produce better learnings. The process of development of a skill culminates when the rational and the emotional motivations are aligned. Then, it can be said that it has eventually turned into a habitual behavior.

Thinking for instance in the delegation skill, for the manager who doesn't have that skill sufficiently developed, it might be very demanding at first to delegate on someone. Undoubtedly, initially, it will have to put in exercise his own rationality, thus contradicting his spontaneous motivation.

Finally, it will come to a point where the manager will perform coaching in a spontaneous way and, besides, will possess the skills to efficiently lead that process. Then it will become a habitual behavior for him. At this point, we will be able to say that the manager has developed the mentioned skill and that he has turned himself into a good "delegator".

Anyway, in his way up to self-development, he will meet obstacles that generally will have to deal with his mental schemes.

MENTAL SCHEMES

The idea spins around how can we achieve all of the above-mentioned actions when someone is already shaped in a specific thinking style. When someone possesses a specific mental scheme, he possesses firm convictions and it is hard for him to find new answers to increasingly diverse and complex tasks.

Coaching can be the process transformer that specifically intends to develop internal skills that allow eliminate the limitations that someone finds in the fulfillment of some fixed tasks.

At the beginning of a coaching process, it's indispensable to have in mind that the results of the same will be directly proportional to the degree of commitment of the protagonist. It's compulsory, therefore, that he considers coaching as being a priority goal for him.

We can help the individual walk that path, in three stages:

1) Creation of a "common ground"

Confidence and comprehension shape the basis of the delicate process of investigating the situation of every person.

Let's remember that, in many cases, the individuals know that they have to change "something" but they do not to know "how" to do it and this situation can confuse and even shame them. It's a question of establishing "rapport" to accompany the individual in his process of transformation.

2) Aspects of the personality directly linked to the limitations we face

How do we achieve that a change remains sustainable throughout time? When in a given situation we act in a specific way we do it because we assign a meaning to that action. Hence, to produce a change implies modifying the meaning that this action has for us. If what's modified is only the instantaneous behavior, after a while the individual resorts to old habits.

Let's see an example. The supposed normal behavior of an employee facing the rebuke of a superior is to lie, in order to try escaping from the possible consequences. However, at a given moment, he decides to modify this behavior; i.e. he chooses not to lie. Nevertheless, it's likely that he could do it in a couple of occasions and later return to the habitual behavior. But, if instead of thinking that accepting his mistake turns out to be dangerous, he contemplates it, for instance, as an opportunity to improve, he will have modified the deep structure that was driving him to lie.

Put that way, it sounds appealing, but obviously it is no that easy.

3) Finally, coaching in a strict sense

When do we learn? We learn when we can estimate the difference between what we want to obtain through a specific action and what happens actually when we take to an end the above-mentioned action and are capable of eliminating the above-mentioned difference.

On the basis of the information obtained during the evaluation, in general, we will work on three aspects helping us achieve that learning:

- Analysis of labor situations through reflexive investigation. This allows us check the perception that the individual has about his own experience and identify the obstacles that prevent the achievement of the desired performance.

- Personal change. This implies the skills development of leadership, communication, negotiation and resolution of conflicts, of creativity, of systemic thinking, etc.
- Incorporation of knowledge for the action, specific knowledge of management.

In synthesis, if we consider the workplace to be full of adventures and uncertainty, what counts is to have resources; and that's, actually, the central function of the processes of coaching: to develop the resources in order that these are available here and now.

Obviously, it implies a resources management strategy different from the classic approach.

New Human Resources

The new reality has modified the implicit contract between the employees and the company. Traditionally, the company was trading safety for a reasonable job. Nowadays, increasingly, the employee looks in the company for a professional development that ensures his future. Meanwhile, the company seeks to promote to the max the skills of its individuals to assure them some future results, although those later nearly always turn out to be quite unspecific.

That way, whereas the former implicit contract was based on the permanency of the employees in the company, the new contract is, or should be, based on his professional development.

Thinking of the legitimate worry of those managers who ask themselves what will happen if their interlocutors leave the company, it's important to think what happens in those cases where he has not trained the above-mentioned personnel and these individuals decide in spite of everything to stay in the company. That could be an even worse option.

What, definitively, turns out to be clear is that in the new management reality, the survival of the company is going to depend on the capacities of his employees to foresee the future and to be prepared for it.

In this new context, the job of the Human Resources department has substantially changed. In the old times, a rather bureaucratic management of the individuals characterized the above-mentioned department. Its role was always reactive, focused on solving problems and "extinguishing fires" in order to obtain some social peace.

Nowadays, the Human Resources department is turning into a strategic department for the company, as its more important resource is, more and more, the individuals who integrate it.

The new Human Resources department has to focus on attracting, selecting, training, valuing and stimulating the employees whom the company believes being the best possibly qualified individuals. Their role, definitively, is much more proactive, and it is demanded from them that they contributes with added value, beside managing and solving the possible social issues within the company. In the context of the new management reality, the human resources department assumes the responsibility for providing the company with the set of skills that it needs to assure its competitiveness.

Many companies evaluate their employees in terms of results or goals. This evaluation approach focus on number of sold units, percentage increase in market share, improvement in profitability or in quality, etc. Many economic perks and bonuses depend on the attainment of these goals that, typically, possess a time horizon of one year. Provided that the goals are easily quantifiable and measurable, the classical yearly employee appraisal can be carried out in a relatively objective way. This appraisal uses to be performed by the direct boss, who acts both as a prosecutor and as a judge, interpreting the objective information in the light of the economic, management or personal circumstances that should turn out to be relevant for each concrete situation.

Evaluation through goals, nevertheless, examines the past results and doesn't necessarily help develop the skills that the company needs for yielding the future results. A appraisal exclusively focused on results can even be counter-productive when it comes to fomenting the skills development, as the individuals tend to worry only about what they immediately obtain, the WHAT, and not about how, the HOW, they obtain it.

So, they are more and more companies interested in evaluating not only the goals, but also the skills that their employees are developing.

In spite of the advantages that represent enriching the traditional process of goals evaluation, this procedure has the potential problem that, mixing realities as different as goals and skills, it may appear as lacking of balance. Those perceptions turn out to be, potentially, very negative for the motivation and the performance of the employees and, obviously, may stifle their creative and innovative capacity.

Measuring skills is much more demanding than measuring goals as skills development needs of a kind of motivation much deeper than just struggling for the year-to-date financial bonus. Thus, it is advisable that they receive a differentiated treatment, both when being evaluated and when being rewarded. To implement this step, it is first needed to understand more deeply what are the skills.

We have already talked about this topic, but let's make sure we have sufficiently made the point.

Throughout the years, the meaning of the term "skills" has been delimited to designate only those observable behaviors that contribute to the success of a task or of a mission or position.

Continuing in line with this definition, it's important to distinguish between two kinds of behaviors: the sporadic ones and those that turn out to be habitual.

Specific sporadic behaviors, like a creative idea, might contribute to a great extent to the success of a task or mission.

Nevertheless, it turns out to be more enlightening to refer to skills only to designate habitual behaviors, due to the fact that this kind of behavior shapes the habits.

Therefore, the skills are those observable and habitual behaviors that make the success of someone in his daily activity or in his function. The skills are objective as they are observable but, at the same time, they are also subjective as the perception of the same depends, to a great extent, on the beholder. This doesn't happen when we talk about quantitative goals, which, by definition, are quantifiable and independent from the individual who gauges them.

For this reason, the evaluation of the skills needs a procedure more complex than the goals evaluation procedure, as it is vital to bear the above-mentioned subjectivity in mind. First, it's obligatory to have a list of skills with clear and specific definitions that can be interpreted in the same way by different beholders. This fact raises the problem of deciding what kind of skill is important to use with the employees of a company.

We will see that some are more important or more relevant than others for helping us in developing coaching programs.

3 - The necessary skills

Kinds of skills

There exist two fundamental kinds of skills that it's important to distinguish: the technical skills or position skills and the management or generic skills. The technical skills refer to those distinctive attributes or features that a specific employee needs at a given workplace. The technical skills use to include knowledge or specific attitudes to achieve a concrete task. For instance, determined positions can require a specific command of English or of computer.

The management skills are those observable and habitual behaviors that make possible the success of someone in his management function. Those skills are more generic and, although every company can emphasize some more than others, they can be studied jointly from the analysis of the management function.

In a nutshell, the management function consists of designing strategies that produce economic value, developing the capacities of the employees and linking them with the mission of the company. A strategy that's achieving economic value impoverishing the capacities of the employees or diminishing their sense of belonging to the company wouldn't be a valid strategy, because, amongst other things, it would debilitate the capacity of the company to obtain economic value in the future. Therefore, the management function includes, besides a strategic dimension, another dimension that we will name intrinsic or internal.

The internal strategy aims at the development of the people heightening their degree of commitment with the mission of the company.

Whereas strategies measure their efficiency through their economic outcome, the internal strategy measures the degree of commitment and confidence of the employees within the company.

From this analysis of the management function, we deduce two kinds of management skills that the manager and then the coach will imperiously need: the strategic skills, which are those skills aimed at obtaining good economic results; and the development skills, which are those precise skills that help develop the employees and increase their commitment and confidence with the company. To those two kinds of management skills, it's interesting to add a few skills that we name as of personal efficiency.

The personal efficiency skills are shaped by those habits that facilitate an efficient relation of the individual with his environment. Those habits refer to balance and to personal development, and to the maintenance of an active, realistic and stimulant relation with the environment. The personal efficiency skills gauge the aptitude for self-direction, indispensable to lead other individuals. For this motive, those skills promote the efficiency of the strategic and development skills and must be considered to be also management skills.

MANAGEMENT SKILLS FOR THE LEADER

It's the group of management skills that addresses the strategic capacity of a manager and his relation with the external environment of the company. For this group we propose the following basic skills:

- **Business vision:** To recognize and to take advantage of the opportunities, the dangers and the external powers that impact on the competitiveness and efficiency of the business.
- **Problems resolution:** To identify the key points of a situation or of a complex problem and to rely on a good capacity of synthesis.
- **Resource management:** To use the resources in the most suitable, rapid, economic and efficient way to obtain the wished results.
- **Orientation to the client:** To answer with readiness and efficiency to the suggestions and needs of the client.
- **Efficient net of relations:** To develop and support a wide net of relations with the key individuals of the company and of the sector.
- **Negotiation:** To obtain the support and the conformity of the individuals and of the groups that influences our area of responsibility.

DEVELOPMENT SKILLS (MORE SPECIFICALLY ORIENTED TO COACHES)

It's the group of management skills that refer to the intrinsic capacity of a manager / coach and to his relation with the internal environment of the company, especially with the persons. For this group, the following basic skills could be:

- **Communication:** To report in an efficient way, both through formal and informal procedures, and to provide tangible information to endorse our observations and our conclusions.
- **Company:** To assign goals and tasks to the individuals suited to perform the task and to plan their follow-up.
- **Empathy:** Active listening, bearing in mind the inner concerns of the people and respecting their feelings.

- **Delegation:** To ensure that the members of our team have the aptitude to take decisions and possess the adequate resources for reaching their goals.
- **Coaching techniques:** To help our interlocutors discover their areas of improvement and develop their skills and professional capacities.
- **Teamwork:** To foment an environment of collaboration, of communication and of mutual confidence between the members of our team and to stimulate them towards the achievement of the common goals.

Skills of personal efficiency (important for both the manager and for the coach)

These skills promote the efficiency of other two groups of management skills, the strategic ones and the development ones.

We propose a list of four basic skills, each of which is split, in turn, in some sub-skills. And at the end of the chapter, a fifth set of complementary skills.

1 - Proactivity

- **Initiative:** To show an enterprising behavior, initiating and supporting changes with tenacity.
- **Creativity:** To generate approaches and innovative solutions to the new problems that we face.
- **Personal autonomy:** To take decisions with our own criterion, not just as a result of a reaction to our environment.

2 - Self-management

- **Discipline:** To do in every moment what we have decided to perform, without giving up, whatever the difficulties.
- **Concentration:** To maintain a high degree of attention, before one o more problems, during a long period of time.

- **Self-control:** To control our emotions and to act in a way adapted to different individuals and situations.

3 - Personal management

- **Time management:** To prioritize goals, programming the activities in a suitable way and executing them in the foreseen time.
- **Stress management:** To maintain our personal balance in front of situations of special tension.
- **Risk management:** To take decisions adapted to situations of great responsibility and with a high degree of uncertainty.

4 - Personal development

- **Self-criticism:** To evaluate often and in depth our own behavior and the reality that surrounds us.
- **Self-knowledge:** To know our strong and weak points, both in the professional and in the personal area.
- **Personal change:** To change our behaviors in order to strengthen our strong points and to overcome our weak points
- **Innovation and development:** Aptitude to modify things, even departing from ways or from situations not previously envisioned, without necessarily an external requirement that triggers it. It implies designing novel and different solutions before problems or situations force us to merely react.
- **Leadership:** compulsory skill to orientate the action of human groups in a specific direction, inspiring values of action and anticipating stages of development of the action for that group. Here the included skills are fixing goals, performing follow-up of the above-mentioned goals and the aptitude to give feedback integrating the opinions of others.

Likewise all of the above-mentioned skills, other concepts will help us appear as a leader inside the company, and eventually, to manage being a respected coach:

5 – Others skills

- **The voice of the client**: Desire to help or to serve the clients, to understand or to satisfy their needs, even those that have not been deliberately expressed. It implies straining for knowing and for solving the problems of the client, both of the final client, to whom the efforts of the company are directed, and of all those who cooperate in the relation company / client, as personnel alien to the company. It's a question of a permanent attitude of bearing in mind the client needs to incorporate this knowledge into the specific way of planning an activity.

- **Orientation to results**: Aptitude to focus all our acts towards the achievement of the expected results, acting with speed and sense of urgency when having to make important, needed decisions to overcome the competitors, to anticipate the needs of the client or to improve the company. It's a matter of a capacity to administer the already established processes in order that they don't interact with the attainment of the awaited results. In the end, fixing challenging goals, above standards, improving and supporting high levels of performance in the overall frame of the company strategies.

- **Planning and company**: Aptitude to determine the goals and the priorities of the business, detailing the action, the timing and the required resources. This includes the instrumentation of mechanisms of follow-up and the checking of information.

- **Negotiation**: Skill to create a propitious environment for collaboration and to obtain lasting commitments that strengthen the relation. Aptitude to direct or control a discussion using "win-win" attitude, planning options to negotiate the best agreements. Basically, it consists of centering on the problem instead of on the person.

- **Development of the individuals**: To help the individuals grow intellectually and morally. It implies a constant effort for improving the training and the development of the people, based on a proper preceding analysis of their needs and of the company's. It doesn't consist of just sending the individuals to training courses, but of a genuine effort for developing them.

- **Empowerment**: To allow power and to give authority to the people, promoting them. It refers to fixing distinctly goals of performance aligned with the personal corresponding responsibilities. To provide direction and to define responsibilities.

  - To take advantage of the diversity (the heterogeneity) of the team members to bring an added value to the business.
  - To combine adequately the situation, the individual and the time.
  - To achieve a suitable integration of the team. The involved individuals share the consequences of the results with all of the team members.
  - To tackle efficient actions to improve the talent and the capacities of the people.

- **Interpersonal communication**: Aptitude to demonstrate a solid communication skill. To inspire others to share information and to value their contributions.

- **Quality of the work**: Excellence in the work. To possess the aptitude to understand the essence of complex aspects, to transform them into practical solutions for the company, both for its own benefit and for the clients' and other involved estates. To possess good capacity of discernment. To share the professional knowledge. To demonstrate constantly the interest of learning.

- **Strategic thinking**: Skill to rapidly understand changes in the environment, opportunities in the market, competitive threats and strengths and weaknesses of our own company When it comes to identifying the best strategic response, aptitude to detect new business opportunities, to perform strategic alliances with clients, with suppliers or, even, with competitors.

- **Teamwork**: It implies the aptitude to collaborate and cooperate with the people. The opposite thing to making it individual and competitive. In order for this skill to be efficient, the attitude must be genuine. It's suitable that the occupant of the position is a member of a group who really works as a team.

- **Resolution of problems**: It's the aptitude to design the solution that will provide an accurate satisfaction to the problem of the client, attending to his needs. It includes the aptitude to design solutions to the problematic of the client not only present, but also future.

- **To persuade**: Aptitude to seduce a client in order that he acquires a product / service that addresses or satisfies a specific need.

- **Initiative**: it refers to the permanent attitude of going to the people. It's a question of the predisposition to act in a proactive way. It implies demonstrating through tangible actions, not only through words.

- **Entrepreneurship**: what defines the entrepreneur is that he looks for change, faces it and takes advantage of it as an opportunity. It does it for himself or for his company. The entrepreneur contributes with his natural spirit of transformation to his daily management task. It possesses initiative and business acumen. He lives and feels the management activity and the business.

The list can seem to be endless, and obviously we cannot dominate all those skills, but the above list gives some hints about the skills that we have to develop. There are thousands of management books that cover them in depth.

What we can see is that a coach doesn't necessarily need to master all of those skills in order to perform at top level. However, if he manages to command sheer management skills as well as pure coach skills, that coach will be a mighty leader, whose power goes beyond the mere personal development of individuals.

But for now, let's return to an aspect related to the credibility of the coach.

Skills transformed into habits

The commitment and the credibility of the leader are essential in order that his people are sure that they head towards a safe haven. Nowadays it's not acceptable in any way that we promise something and, the following day, betray the promise. Well, provided that we want to be deemed as a real leader.

The leader must develop, beside his own personal vision, a vision of the reason he wants to share it with all his followers as a tool to establish direction to his actions towards the proposed goal. The leader must "walk the talk", inside a frame of permanent visibility, in order that this way the whole world is sure of the consistency of what he preaches.

As a guide in charge of promoting his people, the leader has to try that in his company is eliminated, or at least reduced, bureaucracy. Only that way it will come to what has been given in naming "horizontal administration" that allows dividing it between its key processes. A new organizational model is demanded for those companies that still work vertically, those where the individuals look and are dependent on the boss instead of looking and being focused on the clients, where too many hierarchical levels obstruct the processes of decision-making and for those where loyalty dwells in positions instead of in the company goals.

Likewise, the real leader should forget all the parameters dictated by the Industrial Revolution and learn how to delegate. Hence, not only might he devote his time to the transcendental intentions of the company but also, in parallel, to increase the self-esteem of his employees, showing them that they also can perform as well as he does. That way, not only a major productivity will be achieved, but also this will achieve the job to turn into one more element towards the self-realization of his people.

Now we are familiar with them. Those habits are:

- **Having a vision:** besides his own life project, the leader bases his actions on a vision he shares with his followers.
- **Fixing goals:** it is clear that prior to reaching the final goal it is compulsory to achieve the intermediate goals, which, beyond confirming the advancement of the project, constitute some opportunities to stimulate and reward the arduous work.
- **Centering on one single thing at the time:** although some individuals are able to consider several projects simultaneously, it turns out suitable to center on only one project at a time, though they might develop in parallel,
- **Walking the extra mile:** it means that it's necessary to go always a step beyond what's required, in order to prepare answers for when comes the future. It's never possible to be satisfied with the already achieved results; there's always something more to be done. It's unavoidable to step out of the comfort zone.
- **Learning:** the discipline for learning is the characteristic of the leader who wants to stress its current importance.
- **Positively managing the relations:** the leader can separate the personal problems from the organizational problems.
- **Positively managing problems:** two kinds of individuals exist: those who see problems in the solutions and those who see opportunities in the problems. Hence, the problems must be managed as the opportunities they represent.

- **Managing time:** provided that the leader acquires great quantity of commitments, he must turn into a real expert in time management.

Actually, we can understand leadership as a process of exercising influence on the people towards the achievement of a goal that's accepted by the followers. The leader has to possess a vision, an attractive dream, which frames a confidence context. According to that, the coaching skills relate to a profile of inspiring leader, whose main tool of management is the training of his interlocutors.

In practice, the companies and the individuals are using the concept of coaching in relation to different initiatives.

Amongst them, it's possible to identify two meanings:

- As process of personal change where someone is orientated by a coach
- As skill that develop those who have some responsibility in the conduction of teams.

The common element of both meanings is the conviction that, before the need for reaching goals as a team, a style of conduction that allows the individuals to learn to learn and to direct their own development turns out to be fundamental. The role of the coach is to generate the conditions for the people to discover new options and successfully innovate.

In that process, the manager takes part in instances of evaluation of his skills and of his potential to face the challenges, both present and future, where he has the opportunity of receiving feedback, of learning new tools and putting them into practice in a personalized form.

The methodologies used in that process are very diverse: detailed analysis of the agenda, review of significant relations and strategies used to solve the conflicts, application of instruments of personality evaluation, skills, interests and personal style, formal skills training with video, feedback and accompaniment to the manager in his work meetings, etc.

This kind of program, although costly in relation with the development of groups, offers big benefits. The manager develops his knowledge in an environment that gives him confidence, what allows him penetrate the comprehension of his own skill levels and, at the same time, exercise the above-mentioned skills consolidating them as habits.

The companies define in different ways their work plans. In multinational companies, it's a frequent practice they assume as being part of standard institutional programs, which are given in agreement to common directives and with predefined stages. In local companies, however, it's not a deeply rooted procedure.

The company specifies what concept of coaching they will use and the related involved skills. For instance...

- **Definition of a development plan and of a communication strategy.** Key step to reduce resistances to change and to involve the participants in the program.
- **Process of skills evaluation.** It allows us define a line that contributes to the points that need major development.
- **Return of information about skills evaluation and formulation of development plans.** It is frequent that the professionals react to the evaluations and appraisals with worry. This is due to the risks, real or perceived, before the fact that exposing some weaknesses could constitute a prejudice for the development of their professional career. Any company that performs evaluations must be clear and consistent and make good use of the information, communicating the results to the participants with total transparency.
- **Development initiatives.** Plans that appear through practice of the learning skill.
- Some possible options are:
  - **Personalized Coaching**. It corresponds to the previously described way where the manager develops an individual learning.

- **Personalized training**. It differs from coaching as it centers on the practice of skills, without exploring other areas as the personal life situation, the career projections, etc.
- **Group development**. Seminars and workshops orientated to providing an experience of standard learning to a group of managers.
- **Rotation of charges.** Assignment to projects. Opportunity to acquire and exercise some specific skills.
- **Results evaluation.** Application of measurement instruments to measure progresses, such as evaluations of performance and 360 degrees.
- **Definition of career options.** After having collected information on its employee's talents, the company is in conditions to adopt better decisions about the assignment to new tasks and, at the same time, orientating the employee in the definition of his own learning goals and development of his career.

Let's see then, in a practical way, how to cross the way towards an operative leadership, where our labor will be sustained as coach. To begin, we have to develop ourselves as leaders.

Several leadership levels

Let's imagine the following situation: you are currently evolving at some specific skill level. Later, we will enter this concept more in depth, but let's use it for now. To illustrate this principle, let's say that, in a scale from one to ten, your leadership capacity is in level six. The evidence is this: the efficiency of your work will never exceed your aptitude to direct and influence your people. Nobody can produce at a higher level than his current leadership level.

In other words, your leadership capacity determines your level of success and the success of those who work with you. Never ever forget that as a coach, most often than not, we will not have direct power on people, and you'll have to rely on some "power" proceeding from your leadership abilities.

So far, it doesn't sound pretty clear, undoubtedly. But the notion we want to introduce now has to deal with the notion of leadership levels, and how, depending on what level is currently yours, you can "extract" more or less from your people.

Exercising leadership doesn't imply being a member of whatever exclusive club reserved to those that were born with that specific gift. The personal characteristics that constitute the raw material of leadership can be acquired. Connect it to the desire of being a leader and nothing will prevent you from improving that skill.

The leadership develops, doesn't show off. Obviously, sometimes a real "born leader" will appear, fine, but even so, in order to remain in the apex, it's important to develop the inner characteristics of leadership.

Let's have a look first at those different leaders. Then we will develop the concept of leadership levels.

1 - The natural-born leader (let's assume we are NOT)

- Is born with leadership qualities
- Has beheld leadership in action through his whole life.
- Through his personal development, he has learned more on leadership.
- He possesses self-discipline that will help him being an even greater leader.

It turns out obvious that three of these four qualities can be acquired.

2 - The leader who has been formed:

- Has seen leadership in action through his whole life.
- Through his personal development, he has learned more on leadership.
- He possesses self-discipline that will help him being a good leader.

Those three qualities are acquired ones.

3 - The latent leader:

- Has seen leadership in action recently.
- Is learning to be a leader through personal development.
- Possesses self-discipline enough to become a good leader.

Those three qualities are acquired ones

4 - The limited leader:

- Has few connections or none with actual leaders.
- Has not received development or this later has been scanty.
- Has the desire to manage becoming a leader.

Those three qualities can be acquired though
And finally...

- The managing leaders are thinkers with a long-term vision that they glimpse beyond the daily problems and the quarterly reports.
- The managing leaders are interested in their companies, without limiting themselves to the reports under their direct responsibility. They want to know how are interrelated all of the departments of the company.
- The managing leaders emphasize the vision, the values and the motivation.
- The managing leaders possess a strong political aptitude to confront the.
- The managing leaders don't accept the "status quo".

Summarizing:

- To know how to perform a task is the achievement of mere labor effort.
- To show others how to achieve; that's the achievement of a teacher.
- To make sure that the job should de done by your people is the achievement of a manager.
- To inspire others to do a better job is the achievement of a leader.

Now we are clear on that, let's analyze the different leadership levels.

Leadership levels

Probably due to the fact that many of us want to be leaders, it sounds very nice, remember our obnoxious former colleague; we often interact emotionally with the definition of leadership. Or maybe because we know, or have known, a leader, or, better put, someone we deem as a leader, for whatever reason, we tend to mime his behavior assuming that leadership is a mere personality trait.

Actually, leadership has to deal with the capacity to influence.

As soon leadership has been defined as the aptitude to influence and develop people, it's important to distinctly have in mind how to do it.

And there precisely takes root the problem. Most individuals define the leadership as the aptitude to reach a position, instead of developing people. Therefore, they seek a position, and when they reach it they think that they have become leaders, like if some transmogrification had happened overnight.

This way of reasoning generates two associate problems: those who are given, a contradiction in its own terms, the "status" of "leader", actually of mere boss, experience, often, the frustration of having few reports; and those who lack those degrees or charges, cannot be deemed as leaders and, for that reason, don't develop leaders' skills, especially influence.

Hence, here we observe a common arising of countless misunderstandings, which often derive into conflicts, open or clouded, those later potentially being the most dangerous.

However, we all exercise influence on other individuals. All of us lead in some areas, whereas in others we're led. In some tangible situation, with a specific group, we find someone who exercises a prominent influence. This individual can be different depending on the group and on the situation. In the case that occupies us, the coach is a leader or, at least, it's important he exercises this role suitably.

The prominent leader of any group can be very easily identified. Observe a bunch of individuals when they gather for a meeting for instance. If something has to be decided, who's the individual whose opinion seems of the most value? Who do people observe when a matter is discussed? With whom do they agree more rapidly? And what's more important; eventually whom do the individuals follow? The answers to those questions will help us discerner the individual who's the real leader of that specific group.

A real leader knows the difference between being a boss and being a leader.

The boss handles his coachees. The leader qualifies them.

The boss depends on authority. The leader, on good will.

The boss inspires fear. The leader inspires enthusiasm.

The boss says "I". The leader says "we".

The boss investigates the responsibility for failure. The leader arranges the failure.

The boss knows how it's done. The leader shows how it's done.

The boss says, "go". The leader says, "let's go!"

In general, it is admitted that different levels of "leadership" exist

LEVEL 1: CONTROL DUE TO FUNCTION OR POSITION (ALSO KNOWN AS FALSE LEADERSHIP)

This is the entry level to leadership. The only influence we possess comes from our position.

Anyone can deal with the "control" function because he has been promoted to occupy a specific position. From this position, he can, obviously, hold authority. Nevertheless, the real leadership is much more than possessing authority, it's something more than following the procedures. Never forget that real leadership consists of turning into the individual whom people will follow.

And the individuals, with complete specificity, won't follow a positional leader beyond his established authority. In such a situation, they will do only what they have to do when there are requested to do it.

So, the positional leaders find difficulties working with volunteers, with coachees and with young individuals. Most of us, we have been taught that leadership is a position, period. Nevertheless, we feel frustrated when we notice that individuals follow us just because of our degrees or position. Our real success depends on our capacity for continuing ascending the scale of the different levels of the leadership.

Level 2: Permission (or relations level)

The leadership blooms with a significant relation, not with more rules.

The "leaders" who are in level 1 (of "position"), often direct through intimidation.

In contrast with Level 1, someone placed in the "level of permission" will direct through interrelationships. The agenda doesn't have to deal with "the law of the fittest" but with the development of the individuals. At this level, time, energy and strategy centre on the needs and on the desires of the person. Those individuals, who cannot construct solid and lasting relations, soon will discover that they are unable to support an efficient and permanent leadership.

Level 3: Production and results

At this level, we see some interesting situations arise. The outcomes augment. The state of mind soars. The needs are attended. The goals are reached. Directing and influencing people becomes agreeable and fulfilling. The problems are solved with a minimal effort. Every individual is orientated towards results. Actually, results constitute the main "raison d'être" of the activity.

A great difference exists between the levels 2 and 3. In the "relations" level, the individuals get together just to be united. In the "results" level, the individuals get together to reach a goal. In other words, they are orientated towards results.

Level 4: human Development (behaviors modification). The leader as a natural coach.

The real leader is recognized because, somehow, his interlocutors now demonstrate a top performance.

A leader is great, not because of his power, but because of his ability to give power to the people. The main responsibility of an employee is to adequately perform his task. The main responsibility of a leader is to qualify others to do the job.

The loyalty to the leader reaches his higher level when the individual who follows the leader has grown personally thanks to guidance given by the latter.

Let's examine with more thoroughness the above-mentioned progression. In level 2, the follower loves the leader; in level 3, the follower admires the leader; in level 4, the follower is faithful to the leader. Why? Because one gets commitment from the people when we help them grow.

Level 5: Personality. The "charismatic" leader

With time, effort, will and training, it is possible to reach this level, though normally it's given by birth is a mixture of communication skills, vision and knowledge. If it's not our personal case, which is what may be expected, before reaching this level, assuming that we reach it, we have to work hard on the preceding levels.

Some additional hints on the leadership levels

- Whenever a change takes place in your job or whenever you join a new group of individuals, you find yourself again at first at the lowest of the 5 levels.
- When someone has reached a given leader level he might not want to perform the sacrifices that the new level would demand, and then his influence begins to decrease.
- Every level reached by the leader or by the coachees will constitute one more reason for the individuals to want to follow him.
- Growth takes place only when efficient changes take place. As it promotes the different leadership levels, changes will turn out to be simpler.

Remember, however, that every level is built on the preceding one and that the ladder will be wobbly and unsafe if we neglect the lower level on which the current one is built. For instance, if we move from a permission (relation) level, to a production (results) level and we stop caring for the individuals who follow us and we stop helping them deliver, then in these individuals might arise the feeling that they are being used. As one moves from a level to another, the leadership with someone, or group of individuals, will be deeper and, at the same time, more solid.

If we manage a group of individuals, obviously, we won't be at the same level with each of them. Each employee needs personalized treatment.

The preceding statement implies saying that not everybody will respond the same way to leadership. We don't want to extend on that specific matter, as it is not the core topic of this book, but we can think of the different models of situational leadership and how they can help us come to face those situations.

Anyway, we present a tentative list of the different characteristics that we must demonstrate before advancing to the next upper level:

LEVEL 1: CONTROL DUE TO FUNCTION OR POSITION (OR FALSE LEADERSHIP)

- Know well of what consists our job (job description).
- Know the history of the company.
- Relate the history of the company to the individuals who are employed by it (in other words, be a team player).
- Accept the responsibility.
- Do your job with a lasting excellence.
- Do more than it's expected from you (contribute with added value).
- Offer creative ideas of change and improvement.

LEVEL 2: PERMISSION (OF RELATIONS)

- Demonstrate a genuine interest for the individuals.
- Make more successful those who work with you.
- Observe through the eyes of other individuals.
- Show more interest in the individuals that in the procedures.
- Accompany other individuals along their path.
- Treat the demanding individuals with empathy.

LEVEL 3: RESULTS

- Initiate and embrace the responsibility for growing.
- Develop and cling to a declaration of intention.

- Make of the job description and of the energy, an integral part of the declaration of intention.
- Develop the feeling responsibility for the results, beginning at you.
- Know and do the things that provide a high remuneration.
- Communicate the strategy and the company vision.
- Turn into an agent of change and detect when it's the opportune moment to perform that change.
- Adopt the demanding decisions that lead to a change.

Level 4: human Development (behaviors modification). The leader as a natural coach.

- Understand that the individuals are your more valuable assets.
- Allow priority to the development of the individuals.
- Turn yourself into a model to be imitated by people.
- Put all your leadership efforts in 20 % of the individuals of the highest level.
- Attract other achievers / producers towards the common goal.
- Be sincere in such a way that this complements your leadership.

Level 5: Personality. The charismatic leader

- Your coachees are faithful and ready to sacrifice
- You have spent years directing and training leaders.
- You have managed to be a statesman / adviser and are beheld by others.
- Your main major satisfaction stems from observing the development and the growth of the people.

Let's examine some elements that might help us in this progression.

COACHING AND CHANGE

An important aspect comes from the fact that if what we say and what we do go in the same line, the results will be consistent. We know that the following statements might sound somewhat cheesy, but why don't we conduct a simple self-assessment and wonder whether we are really free of guilt. For instance:

- If I tell my employees: "it is demanded to be punctual", I have to be the first one in respecting this premise. That way, they will also, hopefully, come at work with punctuality. But, if we tell them "it's compulsory to be punctual" and we arrive late at work, the employees will see an absence of consistency between our words and our actions.

- If I stress before the employees: "it's important to be positive", I must be the first amongst them who holds and demonstrates a positive attitude. That way, they will tend to have a positive attitude. If we tell them: "it's important to be positive", and then show a negative attitude we won't be acting in a consistent way before them.

- If I insist and say: "Always place the client first". I must be the first who actually considers the client as the key to success. Doing it that way, the coachees will tend to place the client first. If one says to the coachees: "it's necessary to place the client first" and we prefer our own caprices and interests to those of the client, the employees will be confused and incredulous with regard to such an affirmation.

- If what one does and what one says are not consistent, the results won't be consistent. And, as a consequence of it, we will tend to produce confusion in the people, firstly, and lack of credibility, ultimately.

Our image has to deal with what people think we are. On the other hand, integrity is related to what we actually are.

The ideal situation is when that both things show consistency. Here exists a debate that voluntarily we will leave opened, in order that everyone answers according to his own criterion and beliefs. One of the main premises when it comes to doing anything is to convey integrity. Ideally, this integrity is real, but if not, and we nevertheless manage to convey this feeling, then it also works. But beware! It is paramount to be cautious: it's not possible to be deceptive to the whole world all the time, remember the famous sentence by Abe Lincoln, so let's be extra careful if we chose the "easy" path. It might work, but maybe just for a while. Well, and obviously, once you have been revealed in plain view, just forget about rebuilding any hint of credibility with your people.

Aim: produce a positive change

Now, let's observe that five of the twelve hereafter enumerated problematic points of a potential leader have to deal with the lack of will to change:
- We don't understand the individuals.
- We lack imagination.
- We have personal problems.
- We cast the responsibility to the people.
- We feel overconfident and self-satisfied.
- We are not organized.
- We mount in rage.
- We don't confront risks.
- We are insecure and are to the defensive.

- We are inflexible.
- We don't have team spirit.
- We resist change.

As soon as the leader has personally changed and has seen the difference between a mere fashionable change and a change that was actually needed, he must turn himself into an agent of change. In this world of rapid changes and discontinuities, the leader must be leading the way to propitiate change and growth, and to show the way of obtaining it. First, he must understand both indispensable requirements to produce a change: to know the technical requirements of the same and to understand the attitude to produce it.

THE LEADER CHANGES, HE CHANGES THE COMPANY

Both requirements are paramount. Nevertheless, most of the times, when change is not fully or successfully achieved it is almost always due to the fact that an inadequate motivation has existed; not to a lack of technical skills.

Change equals growth

It seems obvious if we underline that an employee, in general, will deal more easily with the technical requirements of change, whereas the leader will tend to deal better with the motivational and attitude requirements that the employees need. Observe the difference: at the beginning, the skills of the leader are essential. No change will happen if the psychological needs of the actors are not adequately understood.

Nothing's more demanding, dangerous or unspecific than introducing changes. Why? The manager deems as his enemies all those individuals who performed well in the pre-change conditions, and sees only as supporters those individuals who might perform well with change.

The resistance to change is universal. It's possible to find it in all classes and cultures. It seizes every generation by the throat and tries to freeze any move towards progress.

Change doesn't begin spontaneously

When the individuals don't hold the paternity of an idea, in general, they resist it, even though it could redound in their own benefit. People don't like the idea of being manipulated. The wise leaders allow their employees to give contributions and to be incepted as part of the change process.

As a general rule, if we're the one who initiates the change process it will be in our favor; whereas if some of our interlocutor imposes it, we will be opposed to it.

Change alters routine

The habits allow us to perform things without thinking very much, and because of it most individuals we are afraid of changes. Beware! Habits don't have any relation with instincts. It's a matter of acquired reactions. They don't happen spontaneously: we create them. First, we shape habits, but then the habits shape us. Change threatens our habits and forces us to think, to re-evaluate and, sometimes, even, and to forget the past behavior.

Change is afraid of the unknown

Change implies sailing through unknown waters and this, obviously, generates insecurity in us. Because of that, most individuals, and that include us, never forget it, feel more comfortable with the old problems rather than with the new solutions.

THE INTENTION FOR CHANGE IS NOT CLEAR

The employees resist change when they discover it through a second-hand source. When a decision has already been taken, the more time happens between the relapse of that decision, the more resistance will be opposed. For this motive, the decisions must be adopted at an as low as possible level. Then, the individual in charge of the decision, given his proximity with the matter, will adopt a decision of more quality and the individuals more directly affected by the decision will know it through a source close to them and to their problematic.

Change is afraid of failure

The remuneration of change is not compared to the effort it needs.

The individuals, in general, won't change until they notice that the advantages of changing overcome the disadvantages of continuing the old way.

The leaders, in some occasions, don't realize that the employees always will ponder the advantages and the disadvantages of change under the light of their personal potential earnings or losses, not under the light of the company earnings or losses.

Normally, the individuals are quite satisfied with things the way they are.

Some changes won't take place if the individuals are stuck in thinking in a negative way.

When the followers don't like the "leader" who supervises change, those negative feelings prevent them from observing change with objectivity. In other words, the individuals contemplate change in a way similar to the way they perceive to the agent of change, in this case, the leader.

The leader can withstand critique

Some leaders resist change, although it seems contradictory in terms. For instance, if a leader has developed a program that, later, has been replaced by another somewhat better, the individual can perceive such a change as a personal assault and, in consequence, react defensively.

CHANGE CAN IMPLY SOME PERSONAL LOSS

When change is imminent, the question we formulate is "*how will it affect me?*" The suitable question would rather be: "*what do I earn with this?*"

In general, inside any company, three groups of individuals exist in relation to change:

1. Those who will lose;
2. Those who are neutral; and
3. Those who will benefit.

Each group is obviously different and it should be managed with sensibility, but also with firmness.

It's important to have in mind that change can be seen as revolutionary, totally different from what has been, or as evolutionary, a refinement of what existed so far. Obviously, it is much simpler to present change as a simple refinement of "*the way we have always been doing*", than as a big, new and completely different situation. When an opportunity for change appears in the company, the individuals can fit into one of the following categories depending on their response:

1. The early adopters are those who recognize a good idea when they see it.
2. Their opinion is respected within the company. Though they didn't originate the idea, they will try to convince other individuals to accept it.
3. The average adopters, the majority.
4. They will answer to the opinions of the people. In general, they are reasonable in the analysis of a new idea, but they are inclined to support the "status quo". They can be influenced by the influencers, leaders actually, whether in positive or in a negative way, of the company.
5. The late adopters, they constitute the last group to support a new idea.

6. Often, they argue against the proposed changes and maybe never manage to express verbally their acceptance. In general, they will adopt changes if most support them.

7. The latecomers, they are always against change.

8. Their commitment is adamantly with the "status quo" and with the past. Besides, pretty often, they will try to generate conflicts inside the company.

Actually, the evolutionary process of a successful change inside the company could be summarized in a series of steps to follow.

- **Step 1. Ignorance**. The employees feel neither a united direction, nor any sense of priorities. They are "in the gloom".

- **Step 2. Information**. General information is provided to the individuals. At the beginning, the ideas of change are not accepted.

- **Step 3. Infusion**. The penetration of new ideas into the "status quo" can produce a confrontation with apathy, prejudices and tradition. The general trend is to focus on the problems rather than on the opportunities.

- **Step 4. Individual change**. The "early adopters" begin to observe the benefits of the proposed change and accept it. The personal convictions replace complacency.

- **Step 5. Organizational change**. Both facets of the matter are discussed. Here is detected a less defensive attitude and a major opening before the proposed changes.

- **Step 6. Clumsy applications**. Some failures and some successes are experienced as change is implanted. The learning process is rapid.

- **Step 7. Integration**. The rejection decreases and the level of acceptance heighten, as people feel an increasing sense of accomplishment and a secondary wave of results and successes.

- **Step 8. Innovation**. The significant results produce confidence and leads people to accept the inherent risks of the process. The result is the appearance of a will to change more rapidly and distinctly.

Nevertheless, we will find some reactions or approaches like those:

Approach: "I reject this idea because it generates a conflict with my values or prejudgments".

Approach: "Well, I understand change, but I cannot embrace it".

Approach: "I agree with the idea but I have reservations about its application".

Approach: "This idea expresses very well what I feel about this matter".

Approach: "I have put into practice this idea now. It's sensational!"

Approach: "Yesterday I gave this idea to someone. So now, the idea belongs to me".

How to make people "buy" change

- We inform the individuals beforehand in order that they have time to think about the implications of change and of how it will affect them.
- We explain the general goals of change, the reasons to perform it and how and when it will be performed.
- Show the individuals how change will benefit them. Act frankly with those employees who could lose something as a consequence of change. Alert them on time and provide them with some help so they can find another job, whether that would be the unavoidable outcome of the process
- Ask to those who will be affected by change, that they take part in all the stages of the process.
- Keep opened the communication channels. Give the employees the opportunity to discuss change. Incite the

individuals to formulate questions, express commentaries and provide feedback.

- Be flexible and adaptable during the whole process. Admit mistakes and incorporate amendments that are deemed as positive.
- Demonstrate at all time your faith and commitment to change. Demonstrate your confidence in the capacity of the employees to implement change.
- Communicate enthusiasm, provide help, and demonstrate appreciation and recognition to those who are performing change.

Assume that change will take place

The question wouldn't have to be "*will we change at some time?*" but, rather, "*when and how much will we change?*" Don't forget that change is permanent.

Keeping up with changes and informing about them constitutes a constant challenge for any leader.

Not every change necessarily implies improvement, but without change we cannot produce improvement.

Change = Growth; Change = Pain

Change represents both the possible opportunities and the potential losses. It is clear that the proposed change turns into a disaster when:

- It's a bad idea.
- The influencers do not accept it.
- It's not presented in an attractive way.
- It serves only the interests of the leaders.
- It's based only on the past.
- They are too many changes and the latter happen very rapidly.

THE COACH AND HIS TOOLS
FOR MOTIVATION

Well, even now everybody is ready for change and actually willing to work differently, it is not enough.

There exist essentially four basic reasons why the individuals don't perform like they should:

- They don't know what they should know.
- They don't know how to do it.
- They don't know why they should do it.
- There are some obstacles out of control.

These four reasons why the individuals don't explore all their potential constitute, undoubtedly, responsibilities associated with leadership.

The first three reasons refer to performing a given task.

The fourth and last reason causes that many individuals cannot reach their all of their potential performance. Problems arise constantly at work, and in all areas. It's obvious that we the individuals don't like problems, we get quickly tired of them and tend to do anything possible to get away from them. This triggers the fact that other individuals take the reins of leadership in their hands and attack the problems or help people solve it. When problems appear, observe with attention where and to whom do the individuals run in search of a solution.

One important challenge for the leader consists in developing the aptitude to recognize a problem before it turns into an emergency.

The fact is that in the conditions of an efficient leadership, a problem rarely acquires gigantic proportions when it is recognized, managed and solved in its initial stages. And who is the person that makes that possible? Here is a fundamental key, that person will be the leader, and at that very moment, that person has somehow marked his "territory"; he is tacitly recognized as a leader.

If this kind of situation tends to repeat, the leader will have some added opportunities to consolidate his leadership. And finally, the icing on the cake; whereas a real emergency occurs, people will "naturally" look into the direction of that very person. This is not a stone-engraved rule, sure, but it gives us a hint of an explanation of why somebody "suddenly" is viewed as a leader at the workplace.

The great leaders, in general, recognize a problem in the following sequence:

- Feel before (intuition) seeing it.
- They begin to think about it and formulate questions (curiosity).
- They assemble information (processing).
- They express their feelings and discoveries with a few colleagues (communication).
- They define the problem.
- They check their resources (evaluation).
- They adopt a decision (direction).
- They convince their interlocutors de follow the newly opened path

And they achieve all of that mainly because of their attitude. Our attitudes constitute an essential element in our daily lives, and they are very important when it comes to directing other individuals. Leadership has less to see with the position than with the disposition. The disposition of a leader is transcendental because he will exercise influence in the way the followers think and feel. The great leaders know that a suitable attitude generates the suitable atmosphere in order that the people answer giving him the best of themselves.

And that's why a coach is a leader; because he will provoke such reactions in his interlocutors.

Our attitudes are then our more important assets.

Without a few adequate attitudes we will never manage to develop all our potential. Our attitudes give us that small advantage over those who think poorly.

A report published a few years ago in the USA revealed that 94 % of all the managers whose companies were included in the Fortune 500, were attributing their success more to the attitude than to any other ingredient.

Recently, a well-known investigation company requested the vice-presidents and the personnel managers of the hundred largest companies of the USA to mention the most important reason for firing an employee.

Their answers are very interesting and emphasize the relevancy of attitude in the business world. These are the reasons they presented:

- Incompetence: 30 %
- Inability to work with others: 17 %.
- Dishonesty or lie: 12 %.
- Negative attitude: 10 %.
- Lack of motivation: 7 %.
- Mistakes or negation to follow instructions: 7 %.
- Other reasons: 8 %.

It's important to emphasize that, though the lack of the adequate knowledge, aptitude, occupies the first place in the ranking, the following five reasons are directly related to attitude topics.

The difference takes root, consequently, in the attitude. The individuals with negative thoughts can start OK, meet a few successes and even win a game. Nevertheless, sooner or later, in general sooner, their attitudes will hamper their personal development.

We are responsible for our attitudes. Our fate will never be determined by some wailing spirit or by relying on some wishful thinking. There's a very famous sentence: *"The pessimist complains about the wind. The optimist hopes that it changes. The leader sets the sails"*.

You must also have in mind the famous model by Stephen Covey: the circle of worry, influence and control. Covey suggests that we forget about what's within our sphere of concern, external factors, which are out of our hands, concentrate on the control circle, ourselves, in order to expand the influence circle, we and the rest of the world.

That way, the attitude of the leader contributes and helps to influence the attitudes of the followers, as leadership is, first of all, influence. The individuals are influenced by attitudes, the same way we are infected by virus.

This law is also applicable to the field of the influence. Even better, the effects multiply with the influence of a leader. Expressing a smile generates many other smiles. Demonstrating ire triggers ire in the people. Few real victims of fate exist. The generous people receive support eventually when the selfish sees it negated.

Precisely one of the secrets of motivation consists of generating an environment where the individuals are free from the influences that de-motivate.

But, what does really motivate the individuals? Abundant theoretical models exist on motivation. Here we use the Herzberg model, simplifying some of its concepts, and without ranking them.

- **To deliver significant contributions.** The individuals want to join a group or seek a purpose for their actions. They need to see that what they do doesn't constitute a wasted effort, but supposes a contribution. The individuals need to verify the value of what they do. The motivation doesn't come only from the activity, but from the desire to come to the final result.

- **To be part of the goal.** The individuals support what they believe in. It motivates them to be part of the process of fixing a goal and that allows them feel important. They like to feel that they are part of something. When they contribute with information, they show interest in the matter. They appropriate it and support it. The participation in a goal generates a team spirit, improves the state of mind and helps everybody feel important.
- **Positive dissatisfaction.** The unsatisfied individuals present a high degree of motivation, because they see the need for an immediate change. They know that something goes wrong and, often, they reckon they have an idea about what could be done; whether that's right or not. The dissatisfaction can inspire changes or instead generate a negative spirit. Thus, it can lead us to apathy or towards action. The key is in canalizing this energy towards an efficient change.
- **Receiving recognition.** The individuals want credit for their personal achievements and praise for their contributions. Providing recognition is another way of thanking people. Personal achievement is a motivator, but it's even greater when someone perceives that achievement and gives it its due value. Recognition is, thus, a way of giving some meaning to personal existence.
- **Have clear expectations.** The individuals feel motivated when they know what they must do and know they can do it well. Nobody wants to enter a vague task or a job which description is unspecific. Motivation appears in a job when the goals, the expectations and the responsibilities are clearly understood. When delegating responsibilities, make yourself sure of allowing people

the necessary authority to perform the task. The individuals explore better when they have control on their work and time.

And, inversely, what de-motivates people? Specific and rigid behaviour standards can be de-motivating. Sometimes, we act in a specific way without realizing the negative influence this has on other people. Let's see some suggestions to avoid this kind of behavior.

- **Don't minimize anybody.** Public critique and aggressive conversations, even those who are performed in a spur of the moment can hurt your interlocutors. We must be alert and sensitive. Taken to the extreme, minimizing or ridiculing somebody can destroy self-esteem and self-confidence. If we have to criticize, remember that nine positive comments are needed to balance a negative sentence.
- **Don't manipulate anybody.** Nobody likes being manipulated or used. Manipulation, it doesn't matter how subtle it is, knocks down, in a relation, the confidence walls. We achieve much more by being honest and transparent that being crafty and cunning.
- **Make of the individuals your priority.** The individuals are our more important resource; so spend some time in knowing them and worrying for them. Stop talking so much and develop the art of listening, especially about what they feel. Your interest, even in insignificant matters will demonstrate your sensibility.
- **Don't discourage personal growth.** Growth is some kind of motivator; therefore stimulate your employees in order that they grow. Give them opportunities to test new things and acquire new skills. We must not feel threatened by the people's achievements, but rather

be very positive and support their victories. Allow your personnel to triumph and allow them to fail.

Weariness in the employees comes from specific actions that the good leaders can avoid "easily".

- Not giving credit to the suggestions.
- Not correcting the motives of complaint.
- Not stimulating.
- Criticizing the employees before other individuals.
- Not asking the employees for their opinions.
- Not informing the employees about their progress.
- Having favoritisms.

Each of the preceding points constitutes an example of how the leader steals or deprives of food the ego of the coachees.

Having a vision as a leader is fine; but it is also necessary to convey it in a proper way.

The vision

Another key word: vision. Without it, the energy abates, the goals are not fulfilled, the personal agendas arise, the production diminishes and the individuals disperse.

The individuals don't follow the dream in itself. They follow the leader who has that dream and who possesses the aptitude to communicate it in an efficient way. Because of that, at the beginning, the leader gives the vision, but in order that this vision grows and provokes an enthusiasm reaction, the leader must assume the responsibility for it.

Four levels of vision exist in the individuals:

1. Some individuals never have it
2. Some individuals have it but they never follow it, they are followers.
3. Some individuals have it and follow it, they are producers.
4. Some individuals have it, move forward and help others share it, they are leaders.

How can it be like that? It turns out that we see what we're ready to see, not what really is. Every successful leader understands this, and that prompts three questions: what do people see?, why do they see it that way? And how can I change their perception?

What you see is, definitively, what you achieve.

The leaders cannot take their interlocutors further from the place where they have arrived. Because of it, the area of the vision must relapse onto the leader. The followers find the leader and then they find the vision. The leaders find the vision and then they find the individuals.

But... *"How do I manage to have a vision for my company?"* The response to this question is crucial. Until we meet it, we will be a leader only nominally.

Though we cannot provide you with a vision, we can explain you the process for building it.

Nevertheless a great difference exists between someone with a vision and a visionary person.

- Someone with a vision talks little but does a lot.
- A visionary does little but he talks a lot.
- Someone with a vision extracts energy from his internal convictions.
- A visionary individual extracts power from the external conditions.
- Someone with a vision continues even though problems arise.
- A visionary stops when the road goes uphill.

Someone without experience conceives a vision in an idealistic way. For that person, the vision alone is sufficient. Ingenuously, that individual projects the vision on others, hoping that the dream does the work without realizing that the vision needs some support. Someone with experience knows that the individuals "buy" the leader before "buying" the vision. The experienced leaders are fully conscious that individuals are changeable and dreams fragile.

Some basic points about vision:

- The leader determines the credibility of a vision.
- The acceptance of a vision is often determined by the fact of presenting it in the opportune time.
- The value of a vision is determined by the energy and guidance that it bears.
- The evaluation of a vision determines the level of commitment of the individuals.

- The leaders who communicate goals to their followers in an efficient way, manage more than those who don't do it.
- The successful leaders "see" simultaneously in three levels:

Level 1. Perception: To see what's currently happening with the eyes of the reality.

Level 2. Probability: To see what will be with the eyes of discernment.

Level 3. Possibility: To see what can be with the eyes of the vision.

A futurist sees only the level 3. A prophet sees only the level 2. A follower sees only the level 1. A leader lives in level 3, directs in level 2 and listens in level 1.

It turns out essential to understand what hinders the vision in level 1. We see things, not the way they are, but the way we are. Because of it, when a vision is blurred, in general, it's not a problem related to the individuals. It exists several kinds of individuals who endanger the company vision and impede the labor of the manager or the coach.

In level 3, we need to wonder how to help the individuals grow up to the dimension of the vision. This implies that the only thing the leader must constantly do … is stimulate the growth of the individuals to the size of the vision as soon as they visualize it.

Also, the leader must look for achievers to integrate the team. Some qualities of the achievers are:

- The achievers are less sensitive to disapproval and rejection.
- The achievers think about the essential thing.
- The achievers center on the task at hand.
- The achievers are not superstitious; they say "that's life".
- The achievers see "the great picture".

- The achievers welcome the challenges hopefully.
- The achievers don't waste their time in unproductive thoughts.

And finally, bear in mind what's suitable to do and say:

- What's expected from everybody.
- That each one will have an opportunity to get out of trouble by himself
- How everybody is achieving it.
- That each one will be rewarded in agreement to his contribution.

And it's important to avoid the following traps:

- Not requesting advice and not helping the team members.
- Frustrating the personal talent by putting emphasis in the rules more than in the skills.
- Not supporting a constructive critique.
- Not developing a sense of responsibility in the team members.
- Treating everybody the same way.
- Not keeping the individuals informed.

The first goal of the leader is to prepare individuals, not to discard them. And, ultimately, many ways and styles exist to achieve it. It is not an exact science.

Different styles

Here we won't go back to the classical theories about motivation, which we understand are a little bit out of he main topics of this book. We will use some shortcuts then, being well aware of the inherent risks.

Each of us possesses a style or a mixture of different styles. Strangely enough, it may be appreciated that a "leader" who possesses a too much-marked style IS NOT a leader. We have already underlined that the "perfect" coach cannot stick to a single style, as the coach, by definition, is many-sided, having to match his coachee's style.

Also, when we are talking about styles, it must be understood what it means: styles are a slightly different thing from behaviors. Although, when seen by an external observer, there might be some confusion. We personally think that we can "play" with different styles, but always within a clear frame of behaviors. This might sound tricky, and actually it is if we don't manage it properly. In order to explicit it a bit, let's have a look at the different styles we can use, depending on specific circumstances.

1 - Rigid style

It's important to use it moderately. After all, the distinctive characteristics of this style seem to be admirable. The leader establishes extremely high standards of performance and he exemplifies them. He is obsessed by making things better and more rapidly and hopes that everybody around him will act the same. He rapidly detects that some persons don't produce what they must and thus demands more of them. If those individuals don't perform at the expected level, he, without any moral dilemma replaces them with individuals who actually can do it. He might think that an approach like this leads to an improvement in the results, but reality is that it doesn't.

In fact, the rigid style destroys the good climate. Many employees feel overwhelmed by the requirements of the manager and, as a consequence of it, their enthusiasm abates. The directives for the task may be clear in the mind of the leader, but he doesn't convey them with clarity, hoping that the individuals know what they have to do.

The game then doesn't consist in trying to do thing following a clear line of action but, rather, in trying to guess what the leader wants. At the same time, the individuals, often, feel that the leader who's adopting the rigid style doesn't trust his people. As a consequence of it, flexibility and responsibility evaporate. The job becomes so focused on the tasks and routine that it ends up being boring.

As for the remunerations, the rigid style doesn't give feedback on how the individuals develop their work or react hastily when for instance he thinks that the employees are late at work. If the leader leaves them alone, the individuals are without any guidance as they are so accustomed that the "expert" is the one who establishes the rules. Finally, the commitment vanishes under the rule of a rigid "leader" because the employees don't know how their personal efforts fit in the overall picture.

When at the head of a team with talent, the rigid style helps finishing a given task on time or even before the established term. And obviously, under pressure, that style can work. Nevertheless, like any other leadership style, this style never has to be used alone.

2 - SOCIAL STYLE

If the rigid leader demands "Do what I say", the social leader exclaims "individuals come first". Actually, this style still spins around the individuals and favors the values of the individuals and their emotions rather than the tasks and the goals. The social leader tries to support the satisfied employees and tries to generate harmony between them. He centers on the construction of strong emotional links and then he takes advantage of the benefits that this approach provokes.

This style also has a notable positive effect on the communication. Individuals like talking. They share ideas and inspiration. This style stimulates the flexibility as the colleagues entrust each other, allowing the constant innovation and the assumption of risk. The flexibility also appears because the social leader, as a father who sets the home rules for a mature teenager, doesn't impose unnecessary structures on how the task must be carried out. He provides the individuals with the freedom of doing their job the way they think it turns out to be the more efficient.

As a way of recognition and rewarding for the well-made work, the social leader offers a generous positive feedback. This feedback has a special power at the workplace because it's slightly common.

Leaving aside the annual appraisal when it exists, most of we individuals are not used to receiving feedback on our daily efforts or, even worse, we only receive negative contributions. This situation implies that the words of the social leader are more motivating. Finally, those leaders are vital in the construction of a sense of belonging. It's possible, for instance, that they invite to an individual chat all of their direct reports. By nature, they are builders of relations.

Now, when the reports need clear instructions to sail through complex challenges, the social leader leaves them without helm. As a matter of fact, if he trusts them too much, this style can drive the group to failure. The leaders determine a vision, establish standards and allow the individuals to know how their work is contributing to the achievements of the group. Alternating this with the protective approach of the social leader a powerful combination might be achieved though

3 - "Manager" style

This leader maximizes the commitment with personal achievements connecting them with the strategy of the company. Once having fitted the individual tasks into a global vision, the leader manager defines standards that spin around the vision. When he provides feedback on the performance, positive or negative, the only criterion is if this performance stimulates the vision. The parameters of success are clear for everybody, as remunerations for instance. Finally, considering the impact of the style on flexibility, a leader manager establishes the final point but he gives the individuals the freedom to innovate, to experiment and to assume calculated risks.

Because of its positive impact, the manager style works well in almost any business action, but it's particularly efficient when the business is adrift. A leader manager establishes a new course of action and "sells" his interlocutors a renewed vision for the long term.

The manager style, despite how powerful it may be, is not adapted for every situation. This approach fails, for instance, when the leader is working with a team of experts or individuals who have more experience that he: they can see the leader as pompous and out of his place.

4 - COACHING STYLE

The leaders who put into gear the coaching style propose their followers challenging topics, even when it means that their tasks are not going to be quickly completed. In other words, these leaders are ready to accept that a small failure in the short term leads to a learning in the long term.

Of all those styles, the coaching style is the one that's used with less frequency. Many leaders state that they have no time, in this high-pressure world, for the slow and tedious work of teaching the individuals and helping them grow. Nevertheless, after the first session, it takes little or practically no additional time. The leaders who ignore this style are alas sacrificing a powerful tool, as its impact on climate and performance is highly positive.

We must admit that a paradox exists in the positive effect of coaching on the business performance because it centers first on the personal development, instead of on tasks immediately related to the job. Anyway, in spite of it, coaching improves the results.

The explanation takes its root in that coaching needs of a constant dialogue and this dialogue is a way of stimulating people. For instance, flexibility. When an employee knows that his boss observes it, with a positive attitude, and he's interested with what he does, he feels free to experiment. After all, this is a sure way of obtaining feedback rapidly and constructively. In a similar way, the constant coaching dialogue guarantees that the individuals know what's expected from them and how their job fits in a strategy or in a wider picture.

The coaching style works well in many business situations, but, for instance, the coaching style works when the employees are conscious of their weaknesses and when they would like to improve their level of results. In an analogous way, this style turns out to be efficient when people know how to develop new skills that can help them progress. In synthesis, it works better with employees that want to be coachees.

In contrast, the coaching style has little or no effect when the individuals, for whatever reason, refuse to learn or change their manners of doing. And, obviously, it fails if the leader lacks the aptitude to helping his interlocutor. The obvious fact is that many managers are not acquainted with this style or, simply put, are manifestly incompetent in it, especially regarding feedback. However, some companies have integrated the positive impact of this style and are trying to turn it into a pivotal skill.

5 - Democratic style

After having devoted some time listening to the ideas of the individuals, the leader generates confidence, respect and commitment. When we allow the employees think about the decisions that concern their achievements, the democratic leader is promoting responsibility and flexibility. After having listened to the worries of his reports, the democratic leader learns how to support them. Finally, as they perceive that they take part in the determination of the standards for the evaluation of success, the individuals who operate under democratic systems tend to be very realistic about of what can or cannot be fulfilled.

Nevertheless, the democratic style possesses also its disadvantages. One of his more exasperating consequences is that there can be endless meetings where ideas are debated without coming up with a consensus, and the only consequence is the scheduling of more meetings. Some democratic leaders use this style for procrastinating crucial decisions, with the hope that a secret solution will eventually appear. The reality is that his interlocutors end up feeling confused and without any leader. This kind of approach can trigger veiled conflicts.

When, then, does this style work better? This style turns out to be ideal when the leader feels insecure about the best direction for moving forward and is in dire need of new ideas and help of the employees' knowledge. Even if the leader has a strong vision, the democratic style works well when in need of fresh ideas to fulfill this vision.

The democratic style, obviously, has much less meaning when the employees are not competent or are not sufficiently informed to provide advice. And, obviously, it is also important to outline that the generation of consensus can turn out to be a dangerous path in times of crisis.

So finally, as probably already hinted, the rigid style is the least efficient style in most situations.

In view of the impact of the rigid style, it is presupposed that it must never be applied.

Actually, the rigid style can be used with extreme caution, in the few situations where it's absolutely imperative, as in a total restructuring. Anyway it's perfectly adequate during a genuine emergency, as an earthquake or a fire. Also it can work with problematic or demotivated employees, once all the consensual styles have failed.

Now, about demotivation and motivation in the employees, it is just heads and tails:

- They feel that they are not recognized or that their work is not praised enough; they don't know how to celebrate success.
- They perceive that their lives are unbalanced, as they invest too much energy in their job and not enough in their personal affairs.
- They feel that it doesn't matter how much they do, it will never be sufficient.

- They prove to be unable to control the quantity or the quality of the task that they are required to perform or the required resources.
- They feel that their bosses are not in touch with reality or that it doesn't matter for them.
- They experience shame on having mentioned personal topics in the work (interests, family, etc.).
- Their state of mind is crestfallen and they say to be exhausted by stress and pressure.
- They spend their time thinking of protecting their own careers rather than in attending their responsibilities.
- They rebel against strictly following the rules and doing only what they are told to do.
- They talk of their dissatisfactions and worries in informal situations (lunches, friends' meetings, etc.), instead of doing it using the formal communication channels.
- They stop feeling well at their workplace and chat about how demanding is their.
- They don't perceive how they can benefit from more hard work.
- They believe that they have little opportunities to progress or that they don't control their careers.
- They feel lost in emptiness or in a routine and overwhelmed by everything they have to do.
- They tend to be cynical towards the new management initiatives and perceive the different programs and initiatives as just another way of making them work even more.

In conclusion, let's be conscious about different styles and their impact if we want to apply when acting as a leader, and more concretely when dealing with others as a coach.

Summarizing the good coach

Final hints, if we want to be a good leader the basic thing that's needed is wanting to be a good leader.

In order to lead, we must convey confidence.

Confidence is the basis for a climate motivator. Through confidence and team spirit, it's simpler for the individuals to develop and heighten their potential and performance in the long term.

Empathy and influence

Empathy settles in self-knowledge and has to deal with the aptitude of listening and understanding the values, the interests and the emotions of the people and, obviously, with acting accordingly so.

Some behaviors that demonstrate empathy are:

- To understand both the strong points and the limitations of the people.
- To know what motivates and what displeases people.
- To perceive and to interpret adequately the non-verbal communication and the emotional tone of the people.

Influence is the aptitude to achieve that people follow a plan or a line of action.

Some behaviors might be:

- Conveying an attractive vision.

- Making an effort to explain things in a way that the individuals can understand them.
- Generating illusion and commitment amongst the team members.

Identify the style best adapted to each situation

Situations where each style turns out to be more efficient:

- **Visionary:** When an accurate vision is needed, in the situations of uncertainty.
- **Coaching:** When it's compulsory to focus on the development of the potential of the interlocutors in the long term.
- **Democratic:** When consensus and participation are needed.
- **Social:** When it's necessary to strengthen links, bring cohesion to the team or manage diversity in critical situations.
- **Helmsman:** In technical areas or amongst already motivated and competent professionals. During the first phase of the vital cycle of a company where growth is the priority.
- **Authoritarian:** When one is forced to change the habits of a company that goes through a critical situation or when we have to face an emergency.

Flexibility of styles

Provided that every style, even the negatives ones, have their usefulness, the key resides in the flexibility of styles. Knowing what style is the most suitable will give us a good reading of the situation.

Nevertheless, the trap is that often we're thinking about realizing a good reading of the situation obviating the obvious: the results and the feedback the environment feed us with.

Develop all of the necessary skills

We manage to be better leaders if we develop our emotional skills, our emotional intelligence. Based on the identification of the style or of the own domineering styles, we can plan a learning plan that makes possible to develop the compulsory skills, to put in gear other styles and, thus, obtain the compulsory flexibility that turns us into some more efficient leaders.

Those skills can develop through personal observation, through feedback from our colleagues and coachees, from readings, from attendance to courses about emotional leadership or, even better, joining a coaching process.

The coach/leader doesn't give orders but he shares goals, he doesn't sanction; he detects, neutralizes and dissolves the obstacles that constantly arise and hamper the performance of the individuals and teams that are under his responsibility.

The essential tools for an efficient coaching are the correct application of the emotional intelligence, the dialogue that shapes the indispensable emotional conscience and the confidence that makes decentralization of authority possible.

Being able to determine the level of emotional conscience of the individuals and the teams constitutes the first skill the coach uses. This emotional current is the one that the coach/leader must learn to orientate.

Here must be developed a great capacity of dialogue, of active listening. This challenge rarely is achieved, as often we don't pay attention to our interlocutor and, as a consequence, we don't listen.

Truth to be said, it takes much less effort directing people through control and fear that through the authority given by confidence.

No doubt, there must be eliminated the dread that generates distrust for the confidence. The real coach/leader is, first of all, a creator, a generator and a confidence architect.

The major percentage of management activity should be devoted to practicing the emotional aptitudes (empathy, flexibility, power of the emotions, active listening, tolerance, etc.) and to motivating the individuals in order that they offer the best of themselves to the company. Human resources are not a given, they are deserved.

And if properly managed, their success will also be the company's success.

SUCCESS

What do we understand as success and what do we understand as facilitating success?

Success is defined by the coachee, not by the coach. In a coaching relation the coachee is who defines what is and what is not success; this way, the coach helps the coachee reach something, success, that the same coachee has defined, with or without the help of the coach.

Facilitating implies that the coach is going to adopt a role where he is going to help his coachee have more possibilities of obtaining success. In counterpart, the individual in charge of this own success is going to be the own coachee, who's going to be the one who's going to take the final decisions.

We talk then of a relation where two or more individuals interact, in a way that one of them helps the other reach his goals.

If we support this context as general criterion, we will contemplate that here exist a series of key points that will allow us evaluate if a relation is or is not a coaching relation.

Firstly, we have mentioned that this relation we call coaching seeks a few goals, successes, which are defined by one of the parts of the relation, which we have called coachee. It turns out to be transcendental to establish this point. The coach doesn't mark the goal of the relation of coaching. The goal is defined by the coachee. The coach facilitates that his coachee reaches the goals that the very coachee has defined.

In this relational frame, we can produce many different possibilities for performance: the coach has innumerable ways of facilitating the success of his coachee; that way, depending on the kind of goals that the latter has defined, the most suitable strategy will then be chosen.

This is the principle of flexibility. The same recipe probably is not applicable to all situations, so the more flexible is the coach when it comes to facilitating that his coachee reaches success, the more success he will encounter as a coach.

Variable is the nature of the goals, of success and how the coachee defines it, and this variability influences the flexibility that the coach must demonstrate in order to be efficient. Another variable is the nature of the coachee, who, as the unique individual he is, with his desires, worries and longings, with a unique way of thinking and of taking decisions, with some convictions on the limits of his world and of his own capacities, requires that we define a proper strategy for progress measurement.

Within that frame, it's not important what are the tools the coach uses to facilitate the success of the coachee. The means are subordinated to the purposes. This allows coaching adopt many different shapes: coaching without transference of experience, coaching manager, telephone-coaching, group coaching, coaching in strategic marketing...

Finally, being pragmatic to the max, it's not that important whether the coach transfers or not his experience, provided that his coachee is successful. It is not relevant whether the coach is someone external contracted by the company or is an internal individual of the entity; it doesn't matter the way how this relation takes place; it doesn't matter the number of individuals who are implied not even the area of application of the process. What really is relevant is that, in the frame of this relation, the coachee reaches success as he has defined it.

In order to identify the best areas of application let's begin with identifying some possible "successes".

A very simple way to do it consists of identifying desired situations, for instance, areas in our life that we think might be better than they currently. The possibilities are vast:

- Someone single may want to share a project of future with someone.
- A businessman without time enough for his family and who wants to find a balance between work and private life.
- A new writer may want to see his first work published.
- An independent professional (e.g. architect, attorney, psychologist, gardener, electrician or lecturer) might want to consolidate a faithful clientele.
- An individual unsatisfied with the way he makes his living might want to perform a change.
- An unbalanced family might want to harmonize its relations.
- An enterprising businessman might want to start a new business.
- A university student can want to improve his skill to publicly expose his thesis.

The possibilities are numerous. What have we now? A set of situations where a few individuals wish a specific change to take place. The above-mentioned change, in turn, constitutes a criterion that we can use for defining what success is: for any given individual, success will be moving from his current situation to his wished situation.

In a coaching process, we must keep our mind opened, as our coachees might come up with some unexpected wishes. However, in the context of a company, a skillful coach will try to make personal wishes be consistent with the company aims.

A short, and real example. A company had a problem with a salesman who was performing poorly. They asked us to conduct a coaching session, before making up their mind about the decision to be taken, basically sack him. We agreed to a conversation with that individual, and after a while, he told us that his real desire was to start a car repair workshop, as his real passion had to deal with fixing and tuning motor engines.

Quite puzzling at first glance, but we started analyzing with him his vision, and the process that could lead him to success. Truth to be said, we needed quite a long time, as obviously, he was reluctant to share his inner feelings.

Summarizing, we managed to make him see, understand and accept that prior to starting with that business of his, there was a series of abilities he had to learn and to hone a bit. And that the perfect structure was within a company like the one he was working for at that time. Namely, dealing with clients, organization, teamwork, finance, etc, all the compulsory skills for a good businessman, were it his business a large computing company or a small repair shop.

Sounds like a fairy tale, but what happened was this: he started performing on top of his team, and two years after our coaching process, had even been promoted to team leader. Maybe one day he will eventually part the company, but so far, his quest for success is perfectly compatible with the company goals.

As you can see, the most important step in that process had to do with listening, with actual and active listening, understanding what's in the head of our interlocutor, instead of projecting our prejudices or being obsessed by the short-term company issue with that person.

4 – Active listening is vital

A late friend of mine, called Larry H., with a several years lasting tenure as president of a large managers association in the USA gave me a good example of the existing relation between active listening and leadership.

Due to his position, throughout his career, Larry had several opportunities of meeting the former US president Bill Clinton when he was invited to official meetings or conferences amongst other prominent businessmen.

An important detail is that Larry was a straight Republican, when Clinton was a Democrat. And nevertheless, whenever Larry came back from his several, albeit lasting just a pair of minutes, encounters, he was a troubled man, as he, reluctantly, had to admit that he actually liked Clinton and admitted he was a great leader.

And it didn't matter how hard he was trying to concentrate and summon all of his negative prejudice against him, once he was chatting with the big man, the same situation repeated again and again. He was seduced by his interlocutor and recognized him as a leader.

You understand that this kind of situation used to profoundly disturb him. But, being a great professional, he coldly analyzed the situation and came to this conclusion, which he shared with me a few years before his passing: *"Even if I recognize all the tricks in the book, what happens is that during the two or three minutes I chat with Clinton, I feel, I really feel, that at that precise moment, I am the most important person on hearth and that everything I am telling him is of the utmost importance for him, and that he is listening to my concerns with all his body and his heart".*

I don't want to prejudge about what Clinton was actually thinking about what Larry was telling him, although I am pretty sure it was not high on his concerns list, but nevertheless because of the active listening skill he commanded he was able to generate those strong and specific feeling and emotions in Larry, theoretically a declared opponent.

So we must devote all the required time to that skill, although first we must make a detour by a few concepts related to "the Being" and "the Saying", concepts apparently bordering on philosophy, but concepts that actually have a significant impact on the way we do listen to people.

Ontological listening

Thinking of my late friend Larry and his chats with Clinton, when somebody ask us about what would be the main quality, whether we had to choose any, to be successful and to be a good leader/coach, we always give the same response: the active listening skill.

If only we had to develop a specific skill, active listening would be the most important.

Nevertheless, at the same time, it probably turns out to be the most demanding to work upon. It's due to reasons deeply anchored in our brains and that have to deal with "mental schemes", or with the way we have of "seeing" things. To have an ontological vision can help us advance in this area.

"Ontological Coaching" (from "onto", the study of the Being) penetrates the ways of "seeing things" and of interpreting the problems individuals, teams and companies may have.

This particular vision of coaching, in general, focuses on the deep comprehension of the "meanings".

For the "ontology of language" approach, individuals and companies are built through language, this later being seen as a coordination of actions to reach goals, based on 3 principles:

1. We don't know how things are. We only know what we observe and how we interpret what we observe. We live in interpretive worlds.

2. Not only do we act in agreement with how we are, we also act in agreement with how we act, in a self-feeding process.
3. The individuals act in agreement with the social systems to which they belong. Nevertheless, through their actions, although determined by those social systems, they can change them.

THE MISSION OF AN ONTOLOGICAL COACH

The central task of a coach consists of facilitating the learning of his client, pivotal skill for change. The key of change, for a coach, resides in being able to identify the reasons and the main emotions of the coachee and in obtaining the transformations that improve his capacity for reflection and action.

In relation to language, the coach tries to understand how the individual thinks about the world and his surroundings, how he refers to the past and to the future and how he generates sense and interprets the daily facts. In the end, those reasons fix the limits of the learning potential and draft some action lines.

Coaches are learning coaches, as they provoke learning experiences their coachees cannot develop by themselves; they observe them in what they do and detect the obstacles in their performance with the intention of showing them what they don't see, thus, to drive them to tackle actions that lead to the wished change. This way, a coach is not somebody who does "more of the same thing", bearing the "feelings of the individuals in mind". He is not even a "mentor" or a "patternmaker", an "older brother" who provides with example. On the contrary, he is someone who helps others remove obstacles, refocus their way of approaching problems and presents them with opportunities to improve their capacity for efficient action.

Areas of change

In many companies, there's an excess of management and a deficit of leadership. "Ontological Coaching" is a way of rescuing the leadership that underlines the fundamental areas of change in the vision of the modern company:

The figure of authority

The traditional model of management is based on the figure of authority. Someone orders, controls, checks and punishes in order that people perform a series of tasks.

If nowadays a major interest exists for "leadership", it's compulsory to remember that nobody does adequately things if he feels forced to. Hence, the essence of the leadership is election, the power "to thrill others" in order that those individuals want to be part of a project. Through salary, we can buy the time of an employee, but we will never acquire neither his commitment nor his aptitude to do exceptional things.

The strategy

The way human beings coordinate actions and communicate for the achievement of results is affected by their strategy. In many companies predominates a counterproductive strategy: dread, distrust, reluctance, resignation, resentment, etc.

That strategy conceals "secret costs" due to the absence of commitment, false commitment, tedium and even resentment. Before the punishment threat, we can undoubtedly achieve that someone performs what's asked from him. He will do it to avoid punishment. But nothing more. We won't manage to modify his behavior by any means.

The companies seen as conversational nets

We converse with clients, at meetings, at workshops and at presentations. We coordinate actions with employees, bosses and peers, etc. Even we have some virtual spaces to talk with others by means of e-mail or through a "chat". This way, the company becomes a "net of conversations" capable of generating new senses, new possibilities and new commitments.

So, conversations don't constitute just another element of the job, they are a pivotal element.

We have to wonder then, what makes us think that the individuals will commit themselves to an order? Let's remember that the traditional company is regulated through control (the figure of authority, the boss). But dread, for an employee, limits his aptitude to innovating, experimenting, facing risks and giving more results. By fear of punishment, he flees from commitment. The key consists in removing that dread and replacing it with confidence and with responsible autonomy.

Self-confidence

We need self-confidence to innovate, to "un-learn", to commit, to differ, to change opinion, etc. This is what ontological "coaching" does: to generate conversations that reveal the mental and emotional models who limit the performance of the individuals, to "un-learn" behaviors that don't serve them and to re-learn some more efficient behaviors.

And it's that every individual has his own frame of possibilities; whose borders in time and space have been expanding with technology.

The ontology is based on the interpretation of the reality. We constitute ourselves as beholders as we choose or distinguish specific fractions of reality, which are translated into language. These perceptions tell us about the kind of beholder we are.

Ontology is not to understand things in themselves, but the different interpretations of things (this topic was already approached in one of our preceding books: "The communication man").

The coach wants to understand the individual through language and its potential for constructing a reality. That way, he wants to give room to a new interpretation of the human phenomenon through the evolution of language: the world changes according to how language does, because the latter allows us unveil new realities. This acquires a lot of importance with the mass media (for instance, nowadays, what we don't see on television, simply doesn't exist for us). Hereafter, the language can have a secret face, what one doesn't express, simply doesn't exist for us.

Let's always bear in mind that we human beings are linguistic beings. We live and develop in all the levels of language, which in return constitutes us.

Language generates existence beyond actions. Reality is not verified in an empirical way but through the language, because it's our only way of knowing.

Because of it, we do especially support the coaching conversation and the importance of active listening, way above talking.

Human communication includes two basic facets: to talk and to listen. Generally, it is believed that it's more important to talk, as this facet seems to constitute the active side of the communication. On the other hand, listening uses to be considered as something passive. Good listening generally is normally seen as a given, why in the world?, and is rarely contemplated as a potentially problematic matter.

While we support our traditional concept of language and communication, we will have problems trying to grab the phenomenon of listening. Even more, we won't be capable of developing the skills needed to achieve a more efficient listening.

Listening is a determinant factor of human communication.

If we closely examine the communication process, we will discover that it rests, principally, not on the talking but on listening. Listening is the fundamental factor of the language, strange as it may seem.

Normally, we suppose that in order to listen to other people we just have to expose ourselves to what they say. That way, we assume that by acting so listening is something that's going to happen in a natural way. Nevertheless, it doesn't turn out to be sufficient.

Opening our ears will just allow us hearing to what we are being told. A far cry from actually listening.

The prevalent idea nowadays is that communication is based on the notion of transmission of information (notion inherited from communication engineering). This latter deals with the communication between machines: between a conveyer and a recipient. This model, despite its usefulness in technical matters of transmission, demonstrates his deficiency when it's used for understanding the human communication. The notion of transmission of information conceals, precisely, the problematic nature of the human being when it comes to listening.

This situation takes place, at least, for two reasons:

When we deal with human communication, senses are basic. The way we make sense of what is said is constitutive of the human communication. And it's also a fundamental aspect of the act of listening.

Our traditional way of approaching human communication implies that human beings communicate between them in a mathematical way. But this kind of communication takes place only when the recipient is capable of reproducing the information that's being transmitted.

However, we, human beings don't possess the required biological mechanisms that allow the process of transmission of information happen the way described by the communication engineering theory.

Actually, we don't possess a biological mechanism that allows us reproduce or represent what really happens in our environment. We don't rely on a biological mechanism that allows us to ensure that our sensory experience (to see, hear, smell, taste, touch) rebuilds into our brains exactly precisely what's out there.

We perceive what our sensory and nervous systems allow us to perceive. That way, the senses we use to perceive our environment are those predetermined by our biological structure.

We can affirm, then, although it sounds somewhat cheesy, that we say what we say but people listen to what they listen; actually, talking and listening are different phenomena altogether.

We insist heavily on it because this aspect if of the utmost importance. Most of the problems we face in a communication process arise from the fact that listening differs to talking. And when what has been said is not listened in the awaited way, people fill this critical gap with personal histories and fantasies or prejudices. This mechanism self-feeds and generates even deeper distortion in the communication process.

So let's be clear on that: hearing and listening is not the same thing. Hearing is a biological phenomenon. It is associated to the aptitude of distinguishing sounds in our interactions with the world.

Listening, in contraposition, doesn't work that way. Although his root is biological and rests in the phenomenon of hear, listening belongs to the sphere of language and is constituted by our social interactions with the people.

What separates listening to hearing is the fact that when we listen, we generate an interpretive world. The act of listening always implies comprehension and, therefore, interpretation. Here precisely resides the active aspect of listening.

The interpretive factor performs such importance in the phenomenon of listening that it's possible to listen even if there are no sounds emitted, and, as a consequence, even if there's nothing said, from a semantic point of view, providing that we can be capable of attributing a sense to something.

From a descriptive comprehension to a generative comprehension of the language

Normally we think that we listen to words. Our aptitude to organize the words in bigger units allows us listening to sentences. In our traditional interpretation, the words name or refer to an object, to an event, to an idea, etc.

It is said that the meaning of a word is its connection with what it refers to. But we cannot always indicate what the word refers to, his meaning being established, commonly, by means of a definition.

This interpretation corresponds to the former supposition that language is a passive instrument for describing reality.

Nevertheless, language is an active process.

When we describe what we observe, we are doing a description and that description is not neutral. It plays a role in our horizon of possible actions. To this we name it the generative capacity of language. The language finally generates reality.

Based on this premise, we will generate a final comprehension different from what the described phenomenon really is. When we listen, we don't listen only to words, we also listen to actions. This fact turns out to be critical in order to understand active listening.

When we listen to an action, we also answer, one way or another, to the question of "why" that action is executed. Or putting it another way, "what" drives someone to say what he says.

We suppose that normally some forethought exists in of someone's actions. The actions appear as some answers to an intention, to a motive. This supposition is one of the foundations of the rationalist tradition. From this perspective, one of the basic factors that allow an action to make sense is its intention.

When we act, and also when we talk and listen, i.e. when we are in conversation, we constitute the "what" we are. And we do the same for the other people.

When we listen, when we actually listen, we listen to the concerns of the individuals. We listen to the why the individuals perform the actions they perform. The individuals who can listen are individuals who allow themselves constantly interpret what other surrounding individuals are saying or doing.

When we listen, we must let people talk, but we must also ask questions. Those who can listen don't accept at once the histories they listen to. Often, they challenge them. They don't keep themselves satisfied with a single point of view. They are always looking for another opinion, examining things from different angles.

When we converse, everything what we say is listened by the other, who makes two classes of histories. Both parts are doing this simultaneously.

The act of listening is based on the same ethics that constitute us as linguistic beings. This is, in the mutual respect, in accepting that people are different from us, and such a difference is legitimate. Mutual respect is essential in order to be able to listen.

When we listen, we place ourselves in a position of accepting the possibility that exist other ways of being, different from ours. This could constitute a definition of empathy.

When we talk, we open ourselves to the possibility of divulging what we are; hence we make our soul accessible.

After having done this we accept the possibility that there exist other particular ways of being, other "individuals", different from ours. To this we refer when we talk about "opening".

On the other hand, we must highlight the fact that we share a common way of being with the individual who's talking to us. This is what allows us understand the actions of the people; understand the individuals who are different from us.

The communicative interaction implies the coordination of actions with our interlocutor. To this we call the context of the conversation.

The context of the conversation is one of the factors that determine our listening level. Usually, this defines what we expect to listen.

Another important factor that affects our listening is the emotional state of the conversation. The emotional state is a distinction through which we demonstrate a predisposition, or lack of, for action.

The meaning that we will give to specific actions and the possibilities that we see as a consequence of them will be completely different depending on the emotional state.

If we're interested in listening, actually we will have to become accustomed to observing, first, our emotional state when we converse and, later, the emotional state of the individual with whom we converse.

It is important to observe the emotional state of the individuals when we begin a conversation. The conversation itself is generating permanently modifications in the emotional conditions in those who take part in it.

To communicate in an efficient way, we must be good beholders of the emotional state of a conversation. Nevertheless, besides conversations, we can also judge the emotional state of the individuals observing their non-verbal language.

If we want to communicate in an efficient way, it's important that we ask ourselves how our personal history can be affecting the way we listen and how the personal history of the individual with whom we're talking can affect his aptitude for listening.

When we talk, not only we coordinate actions with other individuals. We also take part in creating an identity in front of the individuals who listen to us. Any thing we say helps generate this identity.

All of this is reflected in the coaching conversations.

Coaching conversation

The coach must control the least possible. The questions that he formulates must be orientated to clarify the vague points or to center the coachee on the treated topic. It's important for him to avoid closed questions.

The closed questions produce brief answers, yes or no, and, therefore, put in danger the control of the conversation. Besides, like most questions, they induce answers of high social acceptance. The opened questions, on the other hand, begin with words as: what, tell me, check, make clear, describe, how, why, which. This kind of questions induces the coachee to talk, they force him probe deeper layers of his reality; they allow to verify suppositions over what the coachee did or how he did it.

During the conversation, it's important to avoid the inefficient questions. This kind of questions is characterized as being predictable, the coachee knows what is the most suitable response, from a social point of view, or theoretical, ridiculous or not related at all to what's being investigated.

The questions we formulate must allow us observe behaviour standards and specific actions, as well as the way the coachee uses to reach his goals.

The most efficient questions are those that seem to be casual, seem simple to answer, and at the same time don't reveal easily what is the concrete aspect that we are currently scrutinizing.

Some of the most common mistakes in conversation relate directly to the formulation of questions.

JD Roman / Manuel Ferrández

Other mistakes can be:

Instantaneous reasons

In 85 % of the cases, the coach makes up his mind even before initiating the conversation. The coach vision is biased because of the physical appearance, the manners, and the small talk before the conversation or because of some information observed in the résumé.

Negative emphasis

The coaches are more influenced by the negative aspects than by the positives.

In fact, the conversation is often a search for negative information and if it is not obtained, the conversation can be considered as deficient. The mistake resides in generalizing, that's to say in finding some negative aspects in the coachee.

Halo effect

The coach tends to overvalue the positive aspects of the coachee and to minimize the negatives. The coach straightforwardly sticks to his own opinions without objectively considering the facts.

Contrast effect

The fact of having a conversation with a coachee exercises a notable influence on the evaluation. This is due to an effect of contrast with other coachees.

Cheap psychology

The coach sees himself as a psychologist and performs completely out of context, and of ethics, interventions and interpretations of the behavior of the coachee

Not taking notes

Taking notes demands a special care, as it must not constitute a distraction for the coachee or for the very coach. Beware, because of confidentiality, the information that's jotted down must not be recorded in any other place.

Other mistakes that are commonly made relate to the phase of planning, if the conversation is not adequately prepared, if we digress or are under pressure for validating a coachee, for instance.

The conversation closing

The penultimate phase of the conversation is the closing. After the conversation has fully developed, that's to say, the goals have been achieved, it's important to start sending signals, generally non verbal, that the conversation is coming to an end.

During that phase, the opportunity is offered to the coachee to clarify his worries with regard to the very conversation or in relation to any aspect of his interest.

It's important to try that the conversation finishes in an agreeable way for the coachee, even though the evaluation of the performance is not favorable.

Finally, it's important to perform a summary of the conversation where the facts observed in the conversation are substantiated and some aspect is corrected if necessary.

In this phase, there are three common mistakes:

1. In the moment of the farewell, allowing the coachee to return on already controversial points. This is especially dangerous.

2. Once formally finished with the conversation, making small talk with the coachee.

3. To finish ahead of schedule. This mistake is obviously due to an inadequate planning and uses to generate uncertainty and disquiet in the coachee.

5 - Final and hints and tips

The contract

The key for an intervention of coaching to be successful begins with this first step: the contract, the establishment of agreements or the design of the alliance

A contract for coaching is similar to a legal contract. It's a matter of establishing a set of clear agreements, assumable on both parts. A contract carefully designed can help clarify the goals of coaching, the approach and, obviously, the results.

In fact, many coaching processes fail due to an insufficient or poorly formulated contract. A contract established with clarity allows that all the parts know at all time where they are and, at the same time, helps the coachee reduce his disquiet and resistance.

To initiate the contract process, the coach must identify with clarity who's the client, what sometimes is not as obvious as it could initially seem, we must identify other relevant parties, for instance, the boss of the interlocutor, in case the coach is not a direct boss, and the needs and desires of all of them, including those of the own coach. In the end, the coach also has some ideas about the conditions that are important to obtaining a good result.

The following step is where the coach assumes the responsibility of making sure that all parts understand and agree with the main terms of the contract. In case of doubt, the best thing is not to presuppose anything. It's much better to insist again with the individuals, even with the risk that they should bother for the iteration, make double-checks and return to the client to confirm our understanding, though we feel that might be deemed as obvious questions, instead of assuming that all the implied is fully understood and agreed.

We recently had a negative experience, with the whole Board of a large company. We didn't spend all the compulsory and unavoidable time on the preparation and validation of the contract, and the whole process went awry, or at least didn't produce the positive outcome that could have been reasonably expected. The main reason is that the Human Resources manager left the company just at the beginning of the process, leaving us orphans of the figure of the project manager, with whom we could have been driving the whole process. We nevertheless decided to plow ahead, although reluctantly, hinting that nothing good could come out of a process doomed since its very birth.

Obviously, there are no miracles; if the steps of the process are not dutifully established before starting with the action, the results will be poor or even negative, beside the fact that getting your wages eventually paid will be quite tricky.

So pay attention and stand firm in your boots when you consider that the process is bent since the beginning. You may lose a contract, but what's the point if at the end you don't get paid anyway?

So, in short, this frame or alliance is the space that encapsulates the coaching process. The interlocutor and the coach design this frame in order that it satisfies the specific needs of every interlocutor.

A large part of the design of the alliance takes place during the initial session between the coach and the coachee.

This frame serves for:

- Creating a safe and valuable space for the interlocutor
- Establishing confidence of the interlocutor in the coach.

- Helping the coach know how to work with the interlocutor in an efficient way, which really provides value to the interlocutor

Obviously, every coach develops his own style throughout the time. Hereafter, we provide some general guidelines that can be of use, having in mind that this first conversation can last from 20 minutes to an hour.

1. Put the interlocutor in context. Coaching offers the opportunity to generate a relation, but it is important to bear in mind, as we have already profusely underlined it in diverse chapters of the book, that this proceeding is relatively novel and, in consequence, the coach will have to help his interlocutors understand what they can expect from the above-mentioned relation.

2. Initiate the design. The coach takes notes and asks the necessary questions to the interlocutor. Specific interlocutors have already an idea of what they would like to do. In this case, it's important to probe a bit.

Some questions that can be formulated to the interlocutor are:

- How do you want that coaching process to be performed?
- What are you looking for in a coach?
- What else?

As the interlocutor provides general answers, it's important to start asking some more specific questions.

- What leads you to leave or postpone tasks?
- What is the best way of addressing you?
- What kind of things would you say about yourself?

In this part of the initial session, it's convenient for the coach to mention what is important for him about the relation that begins now.

It would be important, for instance, for the coach to unveil that he has such or such style, i.e. a direct speech, that he will call things by their name, etc.

In this first phase, we must look relaxed and opened with the coachee, to prove we are sincere and ready to reveal opinions, preferences or feelings in relation with the interlocutor. It's transcendental to have the aptitude to act "directly", of being clear when it comes to establishing the mutual expectations and demanding that the interlocutors are responsible for their actions and consistent with their commitments

In any case, it's important always to remind the interlocutor that coaching is a constant process and that probably this established frame would have to be re-designed as the relation is moving forward.

The four phases according
on the G.R.O.W. model

1 – Goal phase

Coaching takes place when the interlocutor is ready to relate to the coach divulging his personal situation without seeking to convince, to seduce or to obtain his approval. The interlocutor begins a conversation that interlaces with the questions of the coach.

The main responsibility of the coach is to search, to poke, to probe deeper. The main tool of the coach is the questions.

As we have already said before, in a coaching process the questions are more relevant than the answers.

In this stage, the labor of the coach consists of helping specify the goal of the coachee and verify its correct formulation.

You ask about the goal:
- What do you want to obtain?
- What would you like to change?
- What is the matter on which you want to work?
- What results do you expect after this session?
- Up to where you want to go and in what level of detail?
- In the long term, what is your goal about this matter? What is the time frame?
- What benefits does bear for you the attainment of this goal?

- What complementary or associate benefits will you obtain?
- Constructing a sensory record of your goal, what will you see when you obtain it?, what will you hear?, what sensations will you have?, how will you feel?
- What intermediate steps can you identify?, what are the temporary frames?
- John, I would like to treat with you the topic ....
- I would like to help Mary to ..., does it seem to you likely that we meet tomorrow?

The doubt maybe is about what areas it is possible to cover during the coaching process with the interlocutor. The response is any area that the interlocutor wants or needs to improve and that is linked to his professional environment, because the coachee might want to work in an area that we don't consider as being capital for developing his professional performance.

Some classical areas can the following ones:

- To practice delegation
- To update regularly your knowledge
- To have a major emotional self-control
- To heighten the aptitude for giving good feedback
- To improve communication with your fellows
- To listen better
- To fix goals
- To deal with conflicts
- To manage time
- To perform productive telephonic calls
- To manage stress
- To improve the interrelationship with other individuals
- To improve assertiveness
- To better motivate his interlocutors
- To organize and to direct meetings
- To plan activities

- To perform public presentations
- To write documents
- To use appropriately some specific computer program
- Etc.

2 - DIAGNOSIS PHASE

This phase is about generating questions in order for the coachee to consolidate all the relevant information about the situation at hand.

Here, the key skill will be to look for personal information that might be useful for the coaching process.

Equally, the aptitude to understand the emotions and feelings of our interlocutor and their meaning will be fundamental.

And, finally, the aptitude to conceptualize, to find connections and guidelines in the information he handles.

Some questions that can help are the following ones:

Situation:
- What's the current situation?
- What are you currently doing?
- How are you doing it now?
- What is the present situation in more detail?
- How does this situation represent a problem for you?
- What worries you?
- Who's the most affected by this topic?
- Who does know your desire of doing something with this?
- There's someone that has control and how much?
- How much control do you personally have on the result?
- What steps and actions have you taken with regard to the matter so far?

- What will happen if you don't change or do this or that?
- What costs has it at short, medium and long term for you not to change?
- What other individuals or areas of your life will be harmed if you don't change or do this?
- What benefits at short, medium and long term will you obtain as consequence of going on with the action?
- Up to this moment, what has stopped you the most?
- You obtain some kind of benefit supporting the current situation the way it is?
- Do you think that something negative will happen if you leave the current situation or change your conduct?
- What obstacles are you going to have to face on the way up?
- What resources do you already have? (Skills, time, money, enthusiasm, will, support ...)
- What other resources will you need? From where will you extract them?

3 - GENERATING ALTERNATIVES PHASE

It's a question of generating a series of alternatives. The coach, at this point, must be capable of helping the coachee generate the maximum possible options, for he will have to stimulate his creativity and challenge his limitations.

Questions:
- How can you focus on the topic?
- What options have you that depend on you?
- Do you have a list of all the alternatives, complete or partial solutions?

- What else can you do?
- What would you do if you had more time, a higher budget or if you were the boss?
- What would you do if you could begin again and with another team?
- What other options have you?
- Which would be some other especially creative options?
- What individual do you think that would be especially prepared to find solutions or alternatives in this situation? What would he do in your place?
- What are the advantages and disadvantages of each of these options?
- Which one would give better result?
- What alternative do you desire the most or do you think that it would be better?
- Which one would be easier?
- Which one does lead you closer to the goal or ideal situation?
- Which would be the most satisfactory for you?

4 - COMMITMENT PHASE

In this last part, the coach must centre on the specification of the commitment for action on the part of the coachee.

Some questions that can help the interlocutor establish his performance plan are:
- What option or options do you choose?
- Up to what point do they satisfy all your goals?
- What are your criteria and metrics of success?
- When are you going to begin and finish each of the steps?
- What can prevent you from performing these actions?

- What will you do to overcome those obstacles?
- Who needs to know about your plans?
- What support do you need and from whom?
- What are you going to do to get the necessary support? When?
- What levels of motivation and commitment (in a scale of one to ten) have you just now with starting with those actions?
- Why is it not a ten?
- What can you do to heighten this level up to level ten?
- What will you do just now? Calling someone? Annotating it in your agenda? What else can help you? How can you guarantee now that you will take forward your action plan?
- Is there any other thing that you would like to share with me now we have finished?

Final words

Believe in the individuals. This it's the essence of coaching. To be sure that our interlocutor is capable of finding himself the answers to his personal challenges.

This circumstance should be sufficient for companies and the managers start practicing coaching with profusion.

In the end, what are the managers paid for?

The development of their interlocutors should be one of the paramount functions of their job. That their interlocutors earn autonomy in the treatment and resolution of the problems, using their own resources. This approach supposes that the manager, in general, "un-learn" what has turned him into a supervisor, successful in the short term, with a strong orientation to the task. He then will discover the real dimension of the human factor and the full comprehension of what role people play in the contribution to results. For the manager, coaching bears, in essence, a new modality of exercising leadership.

The mental models, the paradigms or the managers internal programming exercise here a critical importance.

The basic belief of coaching is that the interlocutor is a creative individual complete and full of resources. The labor of the manager is, thus, to liberate and to put into gear those very resources. A series of skills contribute to it. The self-management is one of the skills key. Self-management is not to project, not to give answers, in order that our beliefs and values don't interact with those of the interlocutor. To give coaching, like exercising leadership, we need to know ourselves very well.

- **Curiosity** is another fundamental skill. It is a matter of a genuine interest for knowing and learning. Here the aptitude to formulate powerful questions turns out to be essential. Questions that really seek to understand, to extend our vision. Questions that don't look for the reasons, the WHY, but instead propitiate understanding. Questions that in sum achieve that the interlocutor extends his vision, what helps him heighten his autonomy.

- **Listening** is an essential skill. Focused listening and global listening. It means hanging and listening to everything. What it's said with the words, what is said by the body? And also what's un-said.

- **Intuition** is an ingredient very much linked to coaching. It requires that the manager is spontaneous, that he says what he thinks or how he feels and that he is afraid neither to be wrong nor to lose his self-esteem. Beyond that, intuition constitutes a very broad route to discovery, the manager must believe firmly that coaching is possible. He must be convinced that the individuals can obtain their own answers.

- **Generating action and learning** is another skill that a good coach develops. Every coaching process must necessarily lead to action. To a tangible, measurable and attainable action on the part of the interlocutor. The coach has to make his interlocutor see the price of his decisions, what he is going to obtain with these actions and at the same time, be patient. Patience is a transcendental skill at this point. But at the same time it's a realistic role, firmly with the feet on the ground and conscious of up to what point the actions generated by the interlocutor help solve the problem.

Coaching is a tool for development in times of great change. And development is the main function of the new managers and leaders. In order to help to the growth of the interlocutor, coaching is much more appropriate than classical management actions. And besides, it constitutes an intelligent way of well investing your time.

Bibliography

ACEVEDO, José Fernando y LÓPEZ GALLEGO, Francisco, *Adelgazamiento organizacional ¿opción de competitividad?*, Editorial UPB, 2000.

ALLES, Alicia, *Elija al mejor guía para el coach*, Ediciones Granica, 2003.

Dirección estratégica de recursos humanos, Ediciones Granica, 2000.

ANDERSON, Rolph E., HAIR, Joseph F. Jr. y BUSH, Alan J., *Administración de Ventas,* McGraw-Hill, 1996.

ANGEL, Pierre y AMAR, Patrick, *Guía práctica del coaching*, Ediciones Paidós.

BELL, Chip R., *Mentoring, haga crecer a sus colaboradores*, Editorial Gestión 2000.

BLANCHARD, Ken, *Las tres claves del empowerment*, Granica, 2004.

BOYETT, Joseph y BOYETT, Jimmie, *Hablan los gurús*, Gestión 2000, 2003.

CANTERA, Javier (coordinador), *Coaching, mitos y realidades*, Pearson Prentice Hall, Madrid, 2003.

DEBORDES, Pascal, *Coaching, entrenamiento eficaz a los comerciales*, Editorial Gestión 2000.

DESSLER, G., *Administración de personal*, Prentice Hall, 1999.

ECHEVERRÍA, Rafael, *Ontología del lenguaje*, Dolmen Ediciones.

ESTEFANÍA, Joaquín, *El poder en el mundo*, Punto de Lectura, 2001.

FERNÁNDEZ, R. y CARROBLES, J., *Evaluación conductual*, Pirámide, 1982.

FELDMAN, Daniel A., *Coaching people toward success in work and life*, Editorial Centro de Estudios Ramón Areces, 2003.

FOUCAULT, Michel, *Vigilar y castigar*, Editorial Siglo XXI, 1996.

GOLDSMITH, Marshall, LYONS, Laurence y FREAS, Alissa, *Coaching, La última palabra en el desarrollo del liderazgo*, Prentice Hall, 2001.

GOLEMAN, Daniel, *Inteligencia emocional en la organización*, Editorial Kairos, 1996.

HANDY, C., *La edad de la sin razón*, Ediciones Apóstrofe, 1993.

HAMMER, Michael y CHAMPY, James, *Reingeniería de la empresa*, Parragón Ediciones, 1995.

HERREROS DE LAS CUEVAS, Carlos, *El coaching: cura, libera y subvierte, tres casos de coaching ejecutivo*, Ediciones Granica.

HURST, D., *El desafío del cambio*, Editorial Temas, 1995.

KOTLER, Philip, *Dirección de marketing*, Prentice Hall, 2000.

KOURILSKY, Francoise, *Coaching, cambio en las organizaciones*, Ediciones Pirámide, 2005.

KUHN, T., *La estructura de las revoluciones científicas*, México, Fondo de Cultura Económica, 1991.

LAUNER, Viviane, *Coaching, un camino hacia nuestros éxitos*, Editorial Pirámide.

LAWLER, E., *High Involvement Management*, Jossey Bass Publishers, 1991.

LAZZATI, S., *El aporte humano en la organización*, Macchi, 1999.

LEIBLING, Mike y PRIOR, Robin, *Coaching: paso a paso, métodos que funcionan.*

LEVY-LEBOYER, Claude, *Gestión de las habilidades*, Ediciones Gestión 2000, 1998.

LOCKE, Christopher, LEVINE, Rick y SEARLS, Doc, *The Cluetrain Manifesto*, Editorial Norma, 2000.

LÓPEZ GALLEGO, Francisco y ACEVEDO, José Fernando, *La reingeniería como opción de competitividad*, Editorial UPB.

LUKES, S., *Power a radical View*, MacMillan Press, 1988.

LOSADA, S., *Selección, contratación e inducción de personal, El manual moderno*, 2001.

MANSILLA, A., *Cómo conversar*, Norma, 2000.

MAYOR, Alberto, *Ética, trabajo y productividad.*

MIEDANER, Talane, *Coaching para el éxito, conviértete en el entrenador de tu vida personal o profesional*, Editorial Urano, 2002.

MINTZBERG, H., *La estructura de las organizaciones*, Editorial Díaz de Santos, 1984.

MORCILLO, P., *La estructura de las organizaciones*, Pirámide, 2006.

NASH, M., *Cómo incrementar la productividad del recurso humano*, Norma, 1995.

PARSLOE, Eric, *Coachees y mentores*, Panorama, 2005.

RHEINGOLD, Howard, *Smart Mobs, The Next Social Revolution*, 1999.

ROMAN J.D., *The communication Man*, Libros en Red, 2005

ROMAN J.D., *The paper bridge*, Libros en Red, 2005

SALAZAR, Tribiño Gilberto y MOLANO CAMACHO, Mauricio, *Coaching* en acción, McGraw-Hill, 2000.

SANDAHL, Phillip, WHITWORTH, Laura, KIMSEY-HOUSE, Karen and KIMSEY-HOUSE, Henry, *Co-Active Coaching: New Skills for Coaching People Toward Success in Work And Life*.

SENGE, Meter, *La quinta disciplina en la práctica*, Editorial Granica, 1995.

SENGER, Jack, SMALLWOOD, Norm y ULRICH, Dave, *Liderazgo basado en resultados*, Edición Gestión 2000, 2000.

SMART, J. K., *Coaching y feedback eficaces, cómo ayudar a nuestros colaboradores a mejorar sus resultados*, Ediciones Gestión 2000.

SOLER, María Rosa, *Mentoring, estrategia de desarrollo de recursos humanos*, Editorial Gestión 2000.

STANTON, William J., BUSKIRK, Richard H. y SPIRO, Rosann L., *Ventas: Conceptos, planificación y estrategias,* McGraw-Hill, 2001.

SUROWIECKI, James, *Cien mejor que uno, la sabiduría de las masas,* Ediciones Urano, 2004.

WEBER, Max, *Economía y sociedad,* Fondo de Cultura Económica, 1993.

WITHMORE, John, Coaching, *El método para mejorar el rendimiento de las personas,* Paidós, 2003.

LibrosEnRed Publishing House

LibrosEnRed is the most complete digital publishing house in the Spanish language. Since June 2000 we have published and sold digital and printed-on-demand books.

Our mission is to help all authors publish their work and offer the readers fast and economic access to all types of books.

We publish novels, stories, poems, research theses, manuals, and monographs. We cover a wide range of contents. We offer the possibility to commercialize and promote new titles through the Internet to millions of potential readers.

Our royalties system allows authors to receive a profit 300% to 400% greater than they would obtain in the traditional circuit.

Enter www.librosenred.com to see our catalog, comprising of hundreds of classic titles and contemporary authors.

www.ingramcontent.com/pod-product-compliance
Lightning Source LLC
Chambersburg PA
CBHW021556210326
41599CB00010B/464